Eating It Up in Eden:
The Oregon Century Farm & Ranch Cookbook

by Richard H. Engeman

Oregon Century
Farm & Ranch
Program

White House Grocery Press
Portland, Oregon

Copyright © 2009 Oregon Agricultural Education Foundation

All rights reserved. No portion of this book may be reproduced—mechanically, electronically, or by any means, including photocopying—without written permission from White House Grocery Press.

Printed in China.

Engeman, Richard H.
  Eating It up in Eden : the Oregon Century Farm & Ranch cookbook / by Richard H. Engeman.
  p. cm.
  Includes index.
  LCCN 2008943019
  ISBN-13: 978-0-978722111
  ISBN-10: 0-978722116

  1. Cookery, American--Pacific Northwest style.
  2. Cookery--Oregon. 3. Century farms--Oregon.   I. Oregon Century Farm & Ranch Program. II. Title.

  TX715.2.P32E54 2009   641.59795
                        QBI09-200008

Book Design by Susan Bard, Portland, Oregon

Front cover
From top right, clockwise
Postcard of Oregon apples, about 1915, author's collection; family dinner table photograph, about 1905, Cultural Images collection; box label, Pinnacle Packing Co., Medford, about 1940, Hillcrest Orchard collection; cover of loganberry recipes booklet, about 1915, author's collection; Hillman's Snowflake Bread recipe booklet, Cherry City Baking Co., Salem, about 1930, author's collection; two women shelling peas, about 1910, Cultural Images collection; Oregon prunes recipe booklet cover, 1909, Willamette Valley Prune Association, author's collection.

Back cover
From top right, clockwise
Box label, Hillcrest Orchard Co., Medford, about 1940, Hillcrest Orchard collection; Tillamook cheese recipes booklet, about 1950, author's collection; Phez loganberry juice recipe booklet, Salem, 1917, author's collection; White Satin Sugar recipe booklet cover, Nyssa, about 1950, author's collection.

ACKNOWLEDGEMENTS

Eating It Up in Eden celebrates the 50th anniversary of the Oregon Century Farm & Ranch Program. It is also a tribute to the 150th anniversary of Oregon statehood. Most importantly, it is a testament to the tenacity and creativity of Oregon's farm and ranch families, and their contributions to the state's rich and deep agricultural heritage.

Eating It Up in Eden came about as a result of discussions by the management board of the Oregon Century Farm & Ranch program in 2008. Board member Kyle Jansson spearheaded the effort, aided by program coordinators Glenn and Judith Mason. Support came also from board members Dale Buck (Tillamook County dairy farmer), Kimberly Dunn (Oregon Department of Parks and Recreation), Larry Landis (Oregon State University), Richard Engeman (public historian), Madeline MacGregor (Oregon Department of Agriculture),and chair Don Schellenberg (Oregon Farm Bureau). The book project was endorsed by the board of the Oregon Agricultural Education Foundation (OAEF), the educational arm of the Oregon Farm Bureau and the home of the Century Farm & Ranch program.

This book could only have happened with the support and assistance of many people. In addition to those noted above, thanks are due to Janice Reed, OAEF director; Kathy Tucker and Harvey Golden, of White House Grocery Press; and book designer Susan Bard. Special thanks to Fran Hendricks and Arlene Kovash of Oregon Women for Agriculture, who helped select and edit the recipes.

Richard H. Engeman

The Recipe Contributors

The recipes in *Eating It Up in Eden* were contributed by members of Oregon Century Farm & Ranch families. We asked for family favorites: the recipes that are favorites today, the recipes that were favorites yesterday. We asked for recipes that exemplified farm and ranch life, such as using local crops like apples and hazelnuts, or were adapted to serve a noonday meal to a haying crew. We also asked who created the recipe, and we asked for any anecdotes or comments about the recipe.

We received more than 200 recipes—way more than we had room for! Some contributors sent in a single recipe, some sent two or three, some sent even more. Regrettably, we could not include all the submissions. The final selection was made by the editor in collaboration with a number of volunteers. The wonderful response to the call for recipes made it clear that families were proud of their association with the Oregon Century Farm & Ranch Program and with their part in the legacy of Oregon farm and ranch life.

Table of Contents

Appetizers, Pickles & Relishes 7

Soups, Salads & Sauces 13

Meats & Main Dishes 23

Vegetables & Side Dishes 37

Breads & Muffins 45

Pies, Cobblers, Puddings & Preserves 53

Cakes, Cookies & Candy 71

Household Tips & Miscellany 95

Oregon's Agricultural History 100

History of Oregon Century Farm & Ranch Program 102

Roster of Original Century Farms & Ranches 105

Index 121

A Mexican worker harvesting tomatoes in Umatilla County during World War II. P12:2397, courtesy Oregon State University Archives

Family dinner table scene, about 1900, somewhere in the West.
Cultural Images collection

About the Recipes

These family-favorite recipes are published as they were submitted, with minimal editing. Be aware that the number of servings will vary between recipes. Some recipes assume a certain level of knowledge of cookery.

Consult a recent standard cookbook such as *Joy of Cooking* for information on safe techniques for canning and preserving foods.

Contributors often provided the name of the recipe's creator, and we have noted this when it was available. We also noted the name of the contributors' present-day farm or ranch if that was provided. For each recipe, the name of the first farm or ranch owner(s) is also given, along with the county and the date of the first land ownership.

Text that is in italics was provided by the contributor about the recipe and the family's farm or ranch.

Several organizations, firms, and individuals sponsored space in the cookbook. Our thanks to these generous supporters of the Oregon Century Farm & Ranch Program.

Love Cake

1 can Humor
Several pounds of Affection
1 pint Neatness
Some holiday, birthday, and everyday Surprises
1 can Running Errands (Willing Brand)
1 can powdered "Get Up When I Should"
1 bottle of "Keep Sunny All Day"
1 can of pure Thoughtfulness

Mix well and bake in a warm oven. Serve to husband on Sundays with an extra large slice, but save some for every day of the year.

Contributed by Roxie Hobart
Josiah Wellington Hobart, Clackamas County, 1905

Recipes from friends and neighbors

Friends and neighbors shared favorite recipes, copying them out by hand on scraps of paper, inserting them in letters, jotting them down from memory on the blank pages or in the margins of published cookbooks.

Collected recipes might be neatly copied and filed on 3x5 file cards, arranged by type of dish, if the cook was of a tidy frame of mind. Other cooks pasted recipes, torn from magazines and newspapers, into old ledgers or textbooks. These often became stuffed with recipe booklets from food companies as well as recipes "not yet" pasted into the book.

Another way of sharing is the community cookbook. Recipes are contributed to the book, which is sold to help raise funds for a school, church, grange, or similar group—much like this book!

Handwritten recipe in Grandma Dora's handwriting. Like many cooks of her time, Grandma kept her recipes glued or inserted loose in an old school textbook. Author's collection

Appetizers, Pickles & Relishes

APPETIZERS, PICKLES & RELISHES

Seed crops

Fescue, clover, sugar beet, bluegrass, alfalfa, ryegrass, and orchardgrass are among the seed crops raised by farmers in such counties as Lane, Linn, Benton, and Marion. As a major export crop, seed has developed since the end of World War II, and by 2006 more than three-quarters of the nation's production came from Oregon.

Green Tomato Relish

1 gallon green tomatoes
3 green peppers
3 red peppers
8 large white onions

Slice or cut all ingredients into pieces. Layer them in a dishpan and sprinkle with sea salt between layers and over the top. Cover and let stand overnight.

Grind everything. Put in a large kettle and add:
¾ cup white sugar
¾ cup apple cider vinegar

Cook until done. Taste and add more sugar or vinegar as needed. Process in small jars.

Note: Follow USDA guidelines for proper sterilization and canning procedures.

Helen Stevens, contributed by Judy Stevens
Robert Stevens, Morrow County, 1904

Novelty postcard, about 1915. Author's collection

Lola Offenbacher's Dill Pickles (Old German Style)

Pack half a canning jar with cucumbers
Put in 2 or 3 heads of fresh dill
Add several cloves of garlic
Add a tablespoon of pickling spices
Add alum—what is on the end of a dinner knife (about ¼ teaspoon)
Finish filling jar with cucumbers

Boil, and pour over the cukes: 1 quart white vinegar, 3 quarts water, ¾ cup canning salt; pour while mixture is boiling.

Top with 1 or 2 fresh grape leaves.

Put lids on jars. They will be ready in about 4 weeks.

This recipe works well with green beans, green tomatoes, and apples.

Note: Follow USDA guidelines for proper sterilization and canning procedures.

Lola Offenbacher, contributed by Valentine Offenbacher
Fred and Minnie Offenbacher, Jackson County, 1898

APPETIZERS, PICKLES & RELISHES

Dill Dip

2 cups sour cream
2 cups mayonnaise
2 tablespoons chopped green onion
2 tablespoons dried parsley flakes
2 teaspoons Beau Monde seasoning
2 teaspoons dried dill weed

Mix ingredients together. Cover. Refrigerate at least 1 day. Goes well with vegetables and chips.

Contributed by Holly Michaels
Lawrence Michaels,
Douglas County, 1898

Roy Spires driving a farm wagon,
Lloyd Spires ranch, Coos County, 1940s.
Debra McCormick collection

Velma Hiatt Laughlin's Pickled Beets

Select small young beets. Boil in water to cover until tender. Cool in cold water and slip off skins. Make a syrup:

2 cups sugar
2 cups water
2 cups vinegar
1 teaspoon allspice
1 teaspoon powdered cloves
1 tablespoon cinnamon

Bring syrup to a boil, add beets and boil for 10 minutes after they return to a boil. Pack into sterilized jars and seal. Keeps very well.

Note: Follow USDA guidelines for proper sterilization and canning procedures.

Velma said that with some recipes the beets turn "funny" but with this one they stay firm and nice.

— Diane Berry

Velma Hiatt Laughlin, contributed by Diane Berry
John and Elvira Teel, Umatilla County, 1893

APPETIZERS, PICKLES & RELISHES

Oyster Dip

2 packages (each of 8 ounces) cream cheese, softened
1 quart cottage cheese
1 can smoked oysters
garlic salt

Blend all ingredients with an electric mixer until smooth. Refrigerate in a covered container. Use as a dip with chips or vegetables.

Helen Jean Speckhart, contributed by her granddaughter,
Joanne (Speckhart) Lowry-Parsons, Speckhart Farms
John Speckhart, Union County, 1904

The dip has been a holiday family tradition from the 1950s until today. Mary (fifth generation) prepared the oyster dip at the county fair at her 4-H favorite food contest.

— Joanne (Speckhart) Lowry-Parsons

Rainbow Dairy Products brochure, Portland and Seattle, about 1925. Author's collection

Soups, Salads & Sauces

We serve this for most holiday dinners.

— Judy Stevens

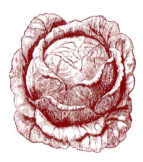

Cabbage-Shrimp Salad

1 head cabbage
1 small onion
½ pound small shrimp
10 to 12 large shrimp
mayonnaise
vinegar
salt and pepper
paprika for decoration

Chop cabbage and onion. Mix mayonnaise and 1 tablespoon vinegar together, enough to moisten cabbage. Add small shrimp and mix. Add salt and pepper to taste. Arrange large shrimp around edge of serving bowl and sprinkle with paprika. Can be adjusted to the size of the crowd by using more of everything. Refrigerate and serve.

Contributed by Judy Stevens
Robert Stevens, Morrow County, 1904

Nano's Mustard Sauce

½ cup tomato soup
½ cup prepared mustard
½ cup vinegar
½ cup butter or margarine
½ cup granulated sugar
3 egg yolks, beaten

Cook together until thickened. Use on ham, in place of mayonnaise in sandwiches, or as a salad dressing.

Vera Schubert, contributed by Betty Schubert
Jacob Schubert, Umatilla County, 1901

Elderberry Soup

Soup

elderberry juice
½ quart pears
sugar to taste

Bring elderberry juice to a boil, add dumplings, pears, and sugar, and cook 15 to 20 minutes.

Dumplings

2 cups water
½ to ¾ cup butter
salt
1½ cups flour
4 eggs

Heat water, butter and salt, then add flour and eggs and cook like cream puffs. Put by spoonful into boiling elderberry juice and cook.

Wilhelmina Hellberg, contributed by Carolyn Hellberg, Hellberg Farms
Christian and Wilhelmina Hellberg, Umatilla County, 1908

SOUPS, SALADS & SAUCES

Judy's Rosa Marina Fruit Salad

1 cup uncooked orzo pasta (looks like fat rice)

Cook the pasta with salt to taste until tender, drain, cool by rinsing in cold water. Set aside.

1 can (20-ounce) crushed pineapple
2 cans (each 15 ounces) mandarin oranges

Drain and set aside; reserve 1½ cups juice in saucepan.

2 eggs, beaten
1 cup sugar (or Splenda)
2 tablespoons cornstarch
¼ teaspoon salt

Add eggs, sugar, cornstarch, and salt to juice in saucepan. Cook over medium heat until mixture thickens. Cool. When cool, stir pasta into sauce, add drained fruits, along with one 10-ounce jar maraschino cherries, drained, rinsed, and cut in half.

Chill overnight. Add whipped topping before serving. Chopped nuts on top is optional.

Contributed by Nancy Cannon
Alice Heller Cannon Coon, Wallowa County, 1884

Bananas are good with an individual serving, but don't do well if there is any left over. This is best chilled overnight but good if used at once.

— Nancy Cannon

Grammy Jane's Buttermilk Salad

3 tablespoons unflavored gelatin
½ cup sugar
⅓ cup fresh lemon juice
2¾ cups buttermilk
2 bananas, diced
1 can mandarin orange sections, drained
1 cup red seedless grapes, cut in half
1 cup crushed pineapple with juice
1 cup whipped cream

Combine gelatin and sugar in a saucepan and stir in lemon juice. Cook over low heat, stirring constantly until sugar is dissolved. Stir in buttermilk and heat a few more minutes. Chill to a jelly-like consistency. Stir in bananas, orange sections, grapes, and crushed pineapple. Whip cream until stiff and fold into fruit mixture. Pour into a pan or mold. Chill until firm. Makes 8 to 10 servings.

> Mary Jane Molthan, contributed by JoAn (Molthan) Silva Summers and Mary Jane Molthan, Malheur County, 1897

Brochure and recipes, Pacific Coast Condensed Milk Co., Seattle, 1915. Author's collection

SOUPS, SALADS & SAUCES

Amanda's Navy Bean Chowder

November 2007 found our dear granddaughter Amanda in a coma in Doernbacher Hospital in Portland. Needing to feed us and wanting comfort food, I adapted this recipe for the crockpot. (Amanda is fine! Thank you, Lord.)

— Paula B. Bangs

1 cup dried navy beans
1 or 2 pieces bacon
1 large carrot, peeled and diced
2 potatoes, peeled and diced
1 onion, thinly sliced
⅓ cup celery, diced
¼ teaspoon pepper
¾ teaspoon salt
3 tablespoons parsley, finely chopped
1 cup milk or light cream
1 tablespoon butter (optional)

Cover beans with cold water and let stand overnight on counter. In the morning, place on low heat and cook gently until soft.

Fry bacon in fry pan. Break up and add with bacon fat to beans, along with prepared vegetables and seasonings. Bring to a boil, then reduce heat and simmer, covered, until very tender. Add light cream and butter, if using. Reheat and serve.

To use this recipe in a crockpot, place all ingredients except milk and butter in crockpot in the morning, cook all day on low. When ready to serve, add milk and optional butter.

Paula B. Bangs, Bangs Family Farm
Frederick and Daisy Bangs, Lane County, 1903

Paula's Butternut Squash Soup

4 or 5 cups butternut squash, peeled and chunked into 1- to 2-inch cubes
4 cups chicken broth (or just enough to barely cover squash)
1 large shallot, minced fine
1 tablespoon butter
½ to 1 cup low-fat sour cream
salt and freshly-ground pepper, to taste
½ cup grated sharp cheddar cheese (optional)
2 pieces bacon, fried, drained and crumbled
green onions, chopped (optional)

Combine squash and broth and bring to a boil. Meanwhile, sauté shallot in butter 5 to 7 minutes, until translucent, and add to the squash. When squash is boiling, cover and turn heat down to low and simmer for 1 hour until squash is very tender.

Using immersion blender (or use regular blender, blending in batches), blend soup until smooth. Add sour cream, salt and pepper, and optional cheese. Stir until cheese is melted, but do not boil. Top with bacon and optional green onions. Serves 4.

Paula B. Bangs, Bangs Family Farm
Frederick and Daisy Bangs, Lane County, 1903

Squash—both summer and winter—grow well in our garden. My husband Larry will only eat so much squash baked with butter and brown sugar, so I invented this soup to try something different and savory, not sweet. It's great light dinner fare with salad and garlic bread.

— Paula B. Bangs

"A flock of white Peking [ducks], about 10 weeks old." Near St. Helens, 1910s. Author's collection

Sauerkraut Salad

1 large can of sauerkraut (don't drain)
1 cup celery, chopped
1 cup green pepper, chopped
1 large onion, chopped

Dressing

1¼ cups sugar
½ cup salad oil
½ cup vinegar

Mix dressing with vegetables and let marinate several hours before serving.

Contributed by Mary Ann Scott
John King, Marion County, 1849

Canning recipes, 1910. Author's collection

Perfect Gravy Every Time

To make the perfect gravy every time start by draining the fat. Add water to the pan you cooked in and let it simmer. Put cold water in another container and add flour and whip until the water and flour are completely mixed. Slowly add the flour and water mix to your simmering pan and mix constantly until mixture boils. Add water to gravy for desired thickness. Season to taste.

Sue Unger, Unger Enterprises
Frank Unger, Washington County, 1906

Summer Garden Soup

1 cup dried navy beans
2½ teaspoons salt, divided
1 small head cabbage, sliced
3 carrots, peeled and diced
1 quart canned tomatoes, undrained
2 white turnips, peeled and diced
1 tablespoon oil
1 onion, thinly sliced
1 large tomato, chopped
½ cup sliced celery
2 tablespoons chopped parsley
1 clove garlic, minced
dash pepper
1 cup spaghetti, broken up

In a 5-quart pot, put the beans with 3 quarts water and 2 teaspoons salt. Cook until beans are tender. Add cabbage, carrots, canned tomatoes, and turnips. Cook 30 minutes longer.

Meanwhile, in a large frying pan, sauté onion and celery in oil for 10 minutes. Add chopped tomato, parsley, garlic, ½ teaspoon salt, and dash of pepper. Cook slowly for 10 to 15 minutes, stirring frequently. Add to the bean mixture along with the broken spaghetti. Cover and cook slowly for 30 minutes, stirring occasionally. Serve, sprinkled with grated parmesan cheese if desired.

Paula B. Bangs, Bangs Family Farm
Frederick and Daisy Bangs, Lane County, 1903

Vegetables

Early Oregon farmers and ranchers had to depend on their own kitchen gardens to provide vegetables for their tables. The development of commercial food preservation methods opened the door to new cash crops for farmers. In the nineteenth century, canneries were the option, while by 1950, frozen foods began to dominate the market. Oregon farmers grow many vegetables—potatoes in Treasure Valley, peas in Umatilla, corn in the Willamette Valley—that are processed for later use. Today, many processors are also creators of food products, such as salsas and stir-fry mixes.

SOUPS, SALADS & SAUCES

Broccoli Salad

2½ quarts broccoli, tops only, cut up
½ cup raisins, chopped
8 pieces crisp bacon, crumbled
½ cup red onion, chopped
1 sweet red pepper, chopped
1 cup unsalted sunflower seeds

Toss with dressing and let sit overnight in refrigerator.

Dressing

1 cup mayonnaise
½ cup sugar
2 teaspoons vinegar
juice of half a lemon, or
 2 tablespoons lemon juice
pinch salt

Avis Cribbins, granddaughter
of Lloyd Spires,
contributed by Debra McCormick,
a great granddaughter
Lloyd Spires, Coos County, 1890

Descendents of Lloyd Spires,
Coos County, 2007.
Debra McCormick collection

Meats & Main Dishes

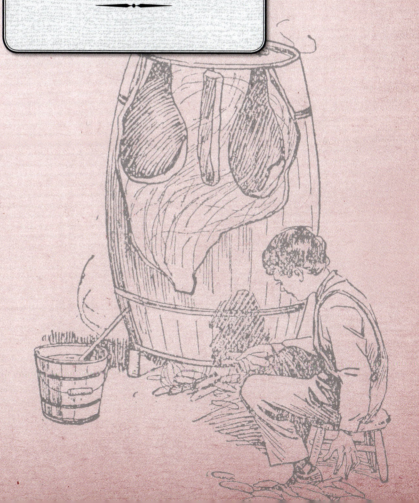

Poultry

Chickens, ducks, geese, turkeys: these always-popular poultry products were also family farm staples. So were their eggs. Turkeys in particular were once big business in Oregon, particularly in the Umpqua Valley and near McMinnville, where the annual "Turkey Rama" began in 1938. Ostriches and rheas joined the farm late in the century, but have remained novelties.

3-Bean Chili in Crock Pot

1 pound ground beef
2 or 3 slices bacon, cut in pieces
1 medium onion, chopped
1 large can pork and beans
1 can kidney beans, drained
1 can butter beans or lima beans, drained
1 cup ketchup
¼ cup brown sugar
2 tablespoons liquid smoke
1 tablespoon vinegar
1 teaspoon salt
dash pepper

Brown beef in skillet with bacon pieces and onion. Drain off fat. Place mixture in crock pot and add remaining ingredients. Stir well. Cover and cook on low for 4 to 6 hours.

Contributed by Nancy Myers
Harry Bartholomew and Charles Bartholomew, Morrow County, 1898

Come and Get It

½ pound wide noodles, uncooked
3 tablespoons chopped onion
1 tablespoon shortening
1 pound ground beef
½ pound pork
2 cups whole kernel corn
1 can tomato soup
1 small can tomato paste
2 teaspoons salt
½ teaspoon pepper
3 cups grated cheese (½ pound)

Boil the noodles in salted water and drain. Brown onion in hot shortening. Add meat and cook until well separated. Add corn, soup, tomato paste, seasoning, and cheese. Put in buttered casserole. Bake at 350°F for 45 minutes.

Frances Schubert Muntinga, contributed by Betty Schubert
Jacob Schubert, Umatilla County, 1901

Frances Schubert Muntinga introduced this to the Schubert family in approximately 1952 and it has without a doubt been the very favorite casserole. I have noticed if you try to substitute or alter ingredients, it doesn't come out the same. However, I do add grated cheese on top and that works fine and tastes great since we are cheese lovers!

— Betty Schubert

Willamette Valley, about 1910. Author's collection

MEATS & MAIN DISHES

Beef Stroganoff

1 pound top round steak
flour
olive oil
onion, medium sized
butter
beef bouillon
salt and pepper
thyme
dill
½ bay leaf
1 cup sour cream
dry mustard
sugar, a pinch
mushrooms, sautéed

This is an old family recipe that has been handed down several generations.

A truckload of hay, Willamette Valley, about 1925. Author's collection

Take 1 pound of top round steak and cut into strips or small squares. Roll in flour and sear in hot olive oil, turning so they are well seared on all sides. Cut a medium sized onion into thin slices and fry in butter until golden brown. Put seared beef and onions in a casserole, preferably earthenware (stoneware). Pour over the mixture enough bouillon to cover, season with salt, pepper, and pinch of thyme, dash of dill, and half of a bay leaf. Put top on casserole and set in a slow (300 to 325°F) oven, allowing contents to simmer gently for at least 2 hours. Can be prepared in the morning and simmered all afternoon. Check periodically and add more bouillon if necessary.

When ready to serve, add 1 cup sour cream, a little dry mustard moistened with water to form a paste, a pinch of sugar, and mushrooms which have been sautéed in butter. Do not allow to come to a simmer again, but serve as soon as it is hot.

Contributed by Shirley Heater
L. D. Heater, Marion County, 1852

Hay Season Round Steak

1 top or bottom round steak (can use any chunk of meat)
1 can cream of mushroom soup
1 cup ketchup
2 tablespoons Worcestershire sauce
1 cup chopped onion

Mix ingredients into a sauce. Put steak into a Dutch oven or casserole, cover with sauce. Bake, tightly covered, in a slow oven. Serves 4 to 6.

Paula B. Bangs, Bangs Family Farm
Frederick and Daisy Bangs, Lane County, 1903

I work right along side Larry during hay season, so noonday dinner needs to take care of itself. This is one of our "standards."

— Paula B. Bangs

Marie Schubert's Ham Loaf

2½ pounds ham, ground
1½ pounds pork, ground
1½ cups cracker crumbs
3 eggs, slightly beaten
2 cups milk
1½ teaspoons savory salt
1½ tablespoons prepared mustard
crushed pineapple (optional)

Mix all ingredients except mustard and pineapple and put in greased pan. Bake 45 minutes in 375°F oven, then cover with prepared mustard and bake 45 minutes longer. Crushed pineapple may be put on top 20 minutes before loaf is done.

Marie Schubert, contributed by Betty Schubert
Jacob Schubert, Umatilla County, 1901

This recipe is famous! Everyone loved Marie's ham loaf and you will too if you haven't tried it. It was served at many a family and community function. We copied the recipe as it was printed in the Valley Herald, the local Milton-Freewater area newspaper.

— Betty Schubert

MEATS & MAIN DISHES

Milk and Cheese

Dairy products have been part of Oregon farming since the first dairy cattle came to Fort Vancouver in the 1820s. Perishability kept most dairy products local until late in the nineteenth century, when milk condensaries, creameries, and cheese factories helped expand markets. Dairy cooperatives prospered in the early 1900s in coastal and valley areas. In 1913, Oregon produced more than 31 million pounds of milk and 3.5 million pounds of cheese. By 2006, milk products were the state's third most valuable agricultural sector.

SUE'S MEXICAN LASAGNA

1 pound ground beef
1 can (32 ounce) tomato sauce
2 packages taco seasoning
1 package corn tortillas
1 can (15 ounce) corn
1 can (15 ounce) black beans
1 can (7 ounce) diced green chiles
2 cans (7 ounce) black olives, sliced
3 cups shredded cheese mix
1 bunch green onions, sliced
1 jar (16 ounce) salsa verde
1 carton (8 ounce) sour cream

Brown ground beef, drain. Add tomato sauce and taco seasoning. Set aside.
Drain and rinse black beans and corn.
In large bowl, combine corn, black beans, green chiles, and black olives.

Using a 9x13 baking dish, layer, in order:

Beef sauce
Corn tortillas (cut to fit)
Sour cream
Salsa verde (to taste)
Bean and corn mixture
Cheese mix

Repeat until dish is full. Bake in 375°F oven for 30 minutes. Top with cheese, bean and corn mix, and sliced green onions.

Contributed by Sue Lewis
Franklin James Lewis, Washington County, 1905

Mom's Mac 'n' Cheese for a Crowd

3 pounds elbow macaroni
1 cube butter (¼ pound)
⅓ cup canola oil
2 quarts milk, heated
1 tablespoon black pepper
2 teaspoons Coleman's dry mustard
1 pound Velveeta cheese
7 cups grated Tillamook cheddar cheese, divided

Cook macaroni until just tender, drain, add butter and oil to noodles, pour heated milk over noodles, add pepper and mustard, stir until butter is melted. Add cubed Velveeta, stir until melted, then add 3 cups grated Tillamook cheddar cheese and stir.

Oil a 20 x 12 x 2½ pan, pour in noodle mixture and then top with remaining 4 cups of grated Tillamook cheddar cheese. Bake at 350ºF for about 1 to 1½ hours, until bubbling and cheese is browned on top.

This makes a massive, farm-sized serving! The proportions can easily be reduced to make a smaller serving.

Lois Root, contributed by Carol Root Seeber
Amos Root, Wasco County, 1878

This is a favorite dish for family picnics and gatherings.

— Carol Root Seeber

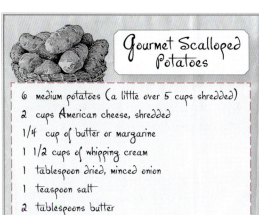

Gourmet Scalloped Potatoes

6 medium potatoes (a little over 5 cups shredded)
2 cups American cheese, shredded
1/4 cup of butter or margarine
1 1/2 cups of whipping cream
1 tablespoon dried, minced onion
1 teaspoon salt
2 tablespoons butter

Cook potatoes in skins and let cool. Peel potatoes and shred coarsely, place in bowl. In a measuring cup add 1 tablespoon of vinegar per cup of whipping cream to sour it. Over low heat, combine ¼ cup of butter and the shredded cheese. Stir occasionally until almost melted and then add the sour cream, onion and salt and heat until cheese is melted. Stir this mixture into the shredded potatoes and pour ingredients into a 2 quart casserole. Dot contents with 2 tablespoons of butter and sprinkle with paprika. Bake, uncovered, in 350 degree oven for 30 minutes.

This space sponsored and the recipe submitted by Don and Judy Schellenberg

MEATS & MAIN DISHES

Bangs Family Breakfast Sausage

1 to 1¼ pounds homegrown fresh ground pork
1½ teaspoon rubbed sage
1 teaspoon kosher salt and ½ teaspoon ground black pepper
   or 1½ teaspoons lemon pepper
½ teaspoon crushed dried red pepper
¼ teaspoon onion powder
½ teaspoon garlic powder

Mix all together with hands. Place in refrigerator and let sit for at least 2 days. Fry in patties, or break up for sausage gravy with white sauce over biscuits.

Paula B. Bangs, Bangs Family Farm
Frederick and Daisy Bangs, Lane County, 1903

Recipe booklet, about 1965.
Author's collection

Impossible Quiche

3 eggs
½ cup Bisquick
½ cup butter or margarine, melted
1½ cups milk
½ teaspoon salt
dash of pepper
1 cup cheddar cheese, shredded
½ cup ham or bacon, cooked and cubed

Place all ingredients except cheese and meat in blender, blend well. Pour into greased 9-inch pie tin. Place cheese and meat over top and push down gently. Bake at 350ºF for 45 minutes. Let set 10 minutes before serving.

Contributed by Holly Michaels
Lawrence Michaels, Douglas County, 1898

Fantastic Five-Hour Stew

2 pounds stew-type meat, chunked and trimmed of fat
3 large potatoes, peeled and cut up in chunks
1 medium onion, cut up in wedges
4 large carrots, peeled and chunked
1 pint green beans, drained
1 cup celery, sliced
¼ cup tapioca, sprinkled over all

Mix all together. Bake, covered, in a 250°F oven for 5 hours.

Paula B. Bangs, Bangs Family Farm
Frederick and Daisy Bangs, Lane County, 1903

Another good noonday dinner when you're real busy.
— Paula B. Bangs

Meat Loaf

3 pounds hamburger (ground beef)
2 medium onions, finely chopped
2 cups oatmeal
3 eggs
2 tablespoons seasoning salt
2 packages Lipton dry onion soup mix
2 tablespoons Worcestershire sauce
1 cup catsup

Place ground beef in a large mixing bowl, make a well in the center and add all the other ingredients. Mix well (I use my hands to mix). When mixed, place in 5-quart ovenproof casserole dish. Bake at 375°F for one hour, or until done.

Lois Root, contributed by Carol Root Seeber
Amos Root, Wasco County, 1878

Beef

The beef industry has been a feature of Oregon life since the overland importation of cattle from California by Ewing Young and other pioneers in 1837. Large-scale beef ranching developed in the Klamath country and southeastern Oregon beginning in the 1870s. Oregon has led the way in the development of specialty rearing and marketing of meat products, such as grass- and grain-fed beef raised without hormones or antibiotics.

Paula's Stir-Fry Peppers, Beef, and Cabbage

1 pound boneless sirloin steak, cut into ¼-inch strips
1 tablespoon minced garlic
½ teaspoon salt
3 cups cabbage, thinly sliced
¼ cup green onions, sliced
1 red, yellow or orange bell pepper, diced
1 cup tomato, diced
hot chili paste, to taste (optional)
hot cooked rice

Sauce

½ cup chicken broth
3 tablespoons soy sauce
2 tablespoons cornstarch

In large, non-stick skillet or wok, sprayed with cooking oil, stir fry the beef, garlic, and salt for 3 minutes. Add bell pepper; stir fry 2 to 3 minutes. Add green onion, tomato, and cabbage and stir fry 2 minutes to wilt cabbage. Mix chicken broth, soy sauce, and cornstarch; add broth mixture to stir fry and boil to thicken. Serve over cooked rice, with or without chili paste. Serves 4.

Paula B. Bangs, Bangs Family Farm
Frederick and Daisy Bangs, Lane County, 1903

Tamale Pie

1 pound ground beef
1 onion, chopped
½ green pepper, chopped
1 clove garlic, minced
1 teaspoon salt
¼ teaspoon pepper
1 cup whole kernel corn
2 cups canned tomatoes
1 can (2.25 ounce) chopped olives
1 teaspoon chili powder
3 cups boiling water
1 cup corn meal

Shucking corn, about 1920. Cultural Images collection

Sauté ground beef, onion, green pepper, and garlic in skillet, breaking meat into bite-size pieces. Add salt and pepper, tomatoes, corn, and olives to mixture. Meanwhile, add cornmeal slowly to boiling water. Cook until thick, then line a greased baking dish with the cornmeal; reserve some for the top. Add meat mixture to baking dish and spread remaining cornmeal on top. Bake at 350ºF for 45 minutes.

To avoid lumps, I always add the cornmeal to some cold water and then stir in the boiling water.

**Contributed by Lucille Kraft
Henry Kraft, Clackamas County, 1904**

MEATS & MAIN DISHES

Seared Sirloin Strips with Dried Tomatoes and Mushrooms

10 dried tomatoes, minced
½ cup boiling water
1 teaspoon salt
½ pound sirloin roast, cut into ¼-inch strips
2 tablespoons butter, divided
2 cups whole mushrooms
1 small onion, cut into thin slices
1 tablespoon minced fresh tarragon
rice or pasta

Re-hydrate the tomatoes in the boiling water and set aside. Over high heat, add the salt to a heavy, medium-sized frying pan. When the pan is well heated, add the sirloin strips. Sear them for 30 seconds on each side, then removed from the pan and set aside.

*Shelling peas, ca. 1910.
Cultural Images collection*

Reduce heat to low and melt 1 tablespoon of the butter. Saute the mushrooms for 3 to 4 minutes until they begin to release their juices, then set aside with the beef. Using the same pan, add the remaining 1 tablespoon of butter and sauté the onions for 5 minutes, or until translucent. Add the tarragon and reserved dried tomatoes, including the water. Let simmer for another 3 to 4 minutes. Add the beef and mushrooms with their juices and cook over medium heat for 5 minutes. Serve hot with rice or pasta. Makes 4 servings.

Contributed by John Wilson
James B. Wilson, Union County, 1889

Verboort Sausage

25 pounds lean pork meat, cubed
¾ cup salt
¼ cup pepper
3 tablespoons allspice

Put pork through meat grinder. Add salt, pepper, and allspice, and mix well with the hands. The sausage can be inserted into casings with a sausage stuffer, or manually with a funnel; it can also be formed into patties. Some sausage makers add a bit of water to the mix.

Bill Unger, contributed by Sue Unger, adjusted by Steve Unger
Frank Unger, Washington County, 1906

Swiss Steak

6 pounds of top sirloin
canola oil
seasoning salt
black pepper
4 medium onions, chopped
garlic, minced
4 tablespoons Worcestershire sauce
1 large can condensed cream of mushroom soup
1½ cups burgundy wine

Flour and season meat with seasoning salt and black pepper. Brown meat in frying pan with canola oil. When meat is browned place in ovenproof pan. Saute chopped onions and garlic in same pan used to brown meat. When onions are translucent, add to meat in pan. Mix mushroom soup and burgundy together and pour over meat and onions. Bake in 350ºF oven for 1 to 1 ½ hours.

Lois Root, contributed by Carol Root Seeber
Amos Root, Wasco County, 1878

This recipe, first written down in 1949, was submitted with formulas for batches of 25, 40, 90, 120, 150, and 180 pounds of meat. The original recipe called for the meat to be ⅔ pork and ⅓ beef, but the Ungers prefer an all-pork sausage.

— Sue Unger

MEATS & MAIN DISHES

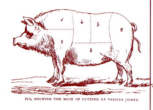

FIG. SHOWING THE MODE OF CUTTING UP VARIOUS JOINTS.

Italian Sausage

25 pounds meat, ground
¾ cup salt plus 2 tablespoons
3 tablespoons paprika
2½ tablespoons crushed hot pepper
3 tablespoons oregano
6 teaspoons coarse black pepper
16 large garlic buds
2 cups vinegar
1 tablespoon cracked fennel seeds
1½ tablespoons cumin

Mix ground meat and other ingredients with the hands. The sausage can be inserted into casings with a sausage stuffer, or manually with a funnel; it can also be formed into patties. Some sausage makers add a bit of water to the mix.

Bill Unger, contributed by Sue Unger, adjusted by Luke Unger
Frank Unger, Washington County, 1906

Bill Unger making sausages, late 1950s.
Irene Unger Fish collection

Vegetables & Side Dishes

VEGETABLES & SIDE DISHES

Onions

~~~~

As a cash crop, onions are relatively new to Oregon. While the fertile lands of Lake Labish near Salem have been noted for their onions for many decades, the onion fields of Morrow, Umatilla, and Malheur Counties have developed since the spread of irrigation systems such as the Owyhee Project (1928-1939). By 2007, dry storage onions were the state's tenth most valuable commodity, and represented more than 20 percent of the nation's production.

Italian Stuffed Cabbage

1 medium head cabbage (about 2½ pounds)
12 ounces sweet Italian sausage links, casings removed
4 ounces ground beef chuck
⅓ cup uncooked regular long grain rice
¼ cup freshly grated parmesan cheese
2 tablespoons chopped fresh parsley
½ teaspoon fennel seed, crushed
¼ teaspoon ground black pepper
½ cup water
1 teaspoon vegetable oil
2 garlic cloves, crushed with garlic press
1 can (14½ ounces) diced tomatoes
1 tablespoon tomato paste
½ cup chicken broth

In a 5-quart stockpot, heat 4 quarts of water to boiling over high heat. Add cabbage to water, cover, and cook about 10 minutes. Transfer cabbage to colander. When cool enough to handle, peel off tender outer leaves, to obtain about 12 large leaves. Trim thick ribs from the base of leaves.

Meanwhile, in large bowl combine sausage, ground beef, rice, parmesan cheese, parsley, fennel seeds, pepper, and water. Mix until well blended, but not overmixed.

Preheat oven to 350°F. In an oven-safe 12-inch skillet, heat oil over medium heat. Add garlic and cook 30 seconds. Stir in tomatoes, tomato paste, and broth. Heat to boiling; reduce heat and simmer 5 minutes.

Place cabbage leaf in ⅓ cup measuring cup and stuff with ¼ cup meat filling. Fold leaf edges over the filling, trimming overhang if necessary. Repeat with remaining leaves and filling. Arrange cabbage packages, seam side down, in skillet with tomato sauce. Cover and bake until cooked through, about 1 hour and 20 minutes. Makes 12 cabbage rolls.

Contributed by Sharon Kerslake
Robert Kerslake, Multnomah County, 1893

Sauerkraut

10 pounds of kraut cabbage, sliced
4 pounds of salt

In a large crock, start layering sliced cabbage and salt. Using a large, clean plate just smaller than the diameter of the crock, weight down the plate, using a large, clean (boiled) rock. Cover top of crock with cheesecloth. Keep crock in a warm corner of kitchen or pantry (preferably about 86°F). Check kraut every few days to see that no mold forms. If you find some, skim it off and discard. Kraut should be ready in about 28 days. When ready, place kraut into 1-quart Ziplock bags and freeze until needed.

Verne Root, contributed by Carol Root Seeber
Amos Root, Wasco County, 1878

Potato Dumplings

10 pounds potatoes
2 cups mashed potatoes, cooked
flour
salt
pepper
butter

Peel potatoes. Grate into mush using lemon peel grater. Strain, using cotton potato sack cloths (not terrycloth). Squeeze out all liquid and discard.

Mix raw potatoes with mashed potatoes and enough flour to make mixture stay together in a ball (about 2 tablespoons). Add salt and pepper to taste. Make into golf ball-sized balls. Boil in salted water for 20 minutes. Serve hot with butter, salt, and pepper. Serves 10 to 15 people.

Contibuted by Francis Etzel
Joseph and Katerina Etzel, Marion County, 1896

VEGETABLES & SIDE DISHES

Recipe booklets from food suppliers

For a hundred and fifty years and more, food suppliers have used recipe booklets to encourage the use of their products. Farm and ranch cooks actively collected them, tearing out favorite recipes or saving the entire booklet. Among the prolific producers of such booklets were millers of flour and grains (regional brands included Crown, Albers, White River, and Fisher), baking soda and baking powder, spices and flavor extracts (Rawleigh and Watkins were national brands), gelatins and cooking oils, condensed milk and canned soups.

Russian Cabbage Rolls

2 heads of cabbage, cored
1½ pounds hamburger
¾ pound pork sausage
1 cup rice, cooked
1 egg
1 medium onion, chopped
3 tablespoons catsup
¼ teaspoon salt
½ teaspoon parsley
¼ teaspoon pepper

Boil cabbage until leaves peel off easily. Trim hump out of stem end of cabbage leaves. Mix all other ingredients and make walnut-sized meatballs. Wrap meatballs in cabbage leaves, one to each leaf. Place torn cabbage leaves in the bottom of a 6- to 8-quart Dutch oven, place rolls on top; put leaves between layers of rolls.

Sauce

½ cup vinegar
½ cup catsup
1 8-ounce can tomato sauce

Cover rolls with sauce. Cover Dutch oven and bake for 2 hours at 300°F.

Ann Davenport Vasconi, Kow Kamp Ranch
Benjamin and Sarah Davenport, Marion County, 1851

The Oregon Farm Bureau is "the voice of Oregon agriculture." It is a voluntary, grassroots, nonprofit organization that represents the state's farmers and ranchers in the public and policymaking arenas. The Oregon Farm Bureau is descended from the Umatilla County Farm Bureau, founded in 1919; the Oregon Farm Bureau was incorporated in 1932.

Among the activities supported by the Oregon Farm Bureau is the Oregon Agricultural Education Foundation, which supports education in the field of agriculture through the Summer Ag Institute, the Memorial Scholarship Program, and the Oregon Century Farm & Ranch Program.

Willamette Farmer: recipes from periodicals

Farm and ranch families added to their repertoire of recipes with contributions from friends and neighbors, and from newspapers and magazines. Recipes had a place in local publications such as the *Willamette Farmer* (1869-1887) and in the newspapers that were published in every town and city. The format for writing recipes was less standardized than it is today. Here are some examples from the *Willamette Farmer* in the late nineteenth century.

Bread Pudding, Without Milk or Eggs
Take one pound of stale bread, a half pound of currants, a quarter pound of sugar and one teaspoonful of ginger. Pour boiling water on the bread and when cool and properly soaked, press out the water and mash the bread, adding the sugar, currants, ginger, a little salt and grated nutmeg, mix the whole well together; put it in a buttered dish, laying a few small pieces of butter on the top, and bake in a moderate over; when baked, let it stand for a few minutes, then turn it out on a flat dish, and serve either hot or cold.

Issue of March 16, 1872

Potato Croquettes
Make a soft paste of finely-mashed potatoes, a little flour, and enough egg to moisten, seasoning with salt. Mould into balls or rolls; dip in beaten egg and then in fine bread crumbs, and fry brown in boiling fat.

Issue of April 9, 1886

Cup Plum Pudding
Take one cup each of raisins, currants, flour, breadcrumbs, suet and sugar; stone and cut the raisins, wash and dry the currants, chop the suet and mix all of the above ingredients well together; then add two ounces of cut candied peel and citron, a little mixed spice, salt and ginger, say half a teaspoonful of each, stir in well-beaten eggs, and milk enough to make the mixture so that the spoon will stand upright in it; tie it loosely in a cloth and put it into a mold, plunge it into boiling water, and boil for three and a half hours.

Issue of April 9, 1886

VEGETABLES & SIDE DISHES

Creamed Peas and Potatoes: Two Versions

Creamed peas and potatoes were clearly a springtime favorite on Oregon farms and ranches. Recipes for it were submitted by Mapril Easton Combs, Carol Root Seeber, and Kathy Spires Larsen (Lloyd Spires, Coos County, 1890). Here are two of them, one from the "wet side" of the Cascades and one from the "dry side." The first is written for an experienced cook, while the second, more detailed, recipe may be more reassuring to novices (but it makes a huge portion!).

This recipe was a family favorite, especially during World War II when my father, Theodore Easton, was off in the Army and my mother, Mildred Neely Easton, was left at home with three young children to raise everything we ate. We had cows and chickens, and sure did not use store-bought frozen peas back then!

— Mapril Easton Combs

Creamed Peas and Potatoes

6 medium potatoes
2 cups fresh peas, or 1 package frozen peas
milk or cream
flour
salt and pepper
butter or margarine

Peel and boil spuds until done. If using new potatoes, scrub skins off first. If using big potatoes, cut in chunks. Cook peas in a little water until just done. Drain potatoes, add to peas, but don't drain peas. Mix a couple of tablespoons of flour into cold milk or cream to make a thin paste, add a little hot water from the peas and stir. Add flour mixture gradually to peas and potatoes; stir to thicken. Add milk or cream until it looks right; add salt and pepper to taste. Add butter or margarine just before serving. If too thin, make up a little more flour paste and add gradually. This is really good made with thick cream and lots of butter.

Contributed by Mapril Easton Combs
Robert and Emma Easton, Coos County, 1898

Grandma Christine's Creamed Peas and New Potatoes

5 pounds new potatoes
4 pounds fresh peas or frozen petite peas
1½ cubes butter
¾ cup flour
1 quart heavy cream
2 quarts milk
salt

Boil potatoes in salted water until tender, drain, and add the peas to the pot while still warm. Make white sauce: combine butter and flour in large microwaveable bowl, add cream and milk, and salt to taste. Microwave on high for 2 to 3 minutes, stir, and continue to cook one minute at a time, stirring after each minute until the mixture begins to thicken. When sauce is finished, pour over peas and potatoes in pot, stir, and serve.

Lois Root, contributed by Carol Root Seeber
Amos Root, Wasco County, 1878

Christine always made this when the new potatoes and fresh peas were ready in the garden. A spring treat!

— Carol Root Seeber

Ad for flapjack flour, Albers Bros. Milling Co., Portland, from the Pure Food Cook Book, published by the Portland Telegram, about 1907. Author's collection

Breads & Muffins

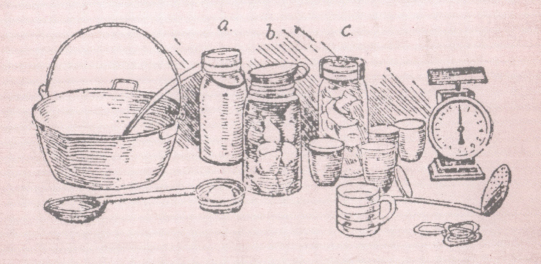

BREAD & MUFFINS

Wheat

Early Oregon settlers usually planted wheat within a few weeks of locating their farmstead. Wheat was legal tender in 1846, and enough was being produced by 1850 to send it to California to feed the influx of gold miners there. Growing wheat in Eastern Oregon began in the 1860s, and the completion of railroads across eastern Oregon in the 1880s encouraged an export market for wheat from that region. By 1914, about 1/7th of the state's crop value was in wheat. Production in 2006 was more than 14 million bushels.

Charlene's Bran Flax Muffins

1½ cups unbleached white flour
¾ cup ground flax seed
¾ cup oat bran
1 cup brown sugar
2 teaspoons baking soda
1 teaspoon baking powder
½ teaspoon salt
2 teaspoons cinnamon
1 cup carrots, shredded
1½ cups apples, peeled and shredded
1½ cups fresh or frozen blueberries
⅓ cup chopped hazelnuts
¾ cup milk
2 eggs, beaten
1 teaspoon vanilla

Mix together and bake in muffin tins at 325°F until done. Sugarless muffins can be made from this recipe, simply substituting 1 cup Splenda brown sugar.

Charlene Haury, contributed by Daniel and Charlene Haury
Jacob and Josephine Stauffer, Marion County, 1892

Swedish Flat Bread (Knäckebröd)

2¾ cups unsifted flour
⅓ cup sugar
½ teaspoon salt
½ teaspoon soda
1 cube butter
1 cup buttermilk

Blend dry ingredients in bowl or food processor. Cut in softened butter until mixture becomes fine crumbs. Stir in buttermilk with fork and mix until it holds together. Shape in a ball with hands. Can be chilled to make it easier to handle. Break off small pieces and roll out real thin to 4 or 5 inches in diameter on floured board, turning over to prevent sticking. Use a fork or Swedish rolling pin to prick the dough in an all-over pattern. Space on ungreased cookie pans. Bake in hot oven (425°F) for 4 minutes until brown. Another method is to bake the knäckebröd on bottom rack on a cookie sheet for 2 to 3 minutes, then slip the bread onto the top rack to finish baking. Keep a close eye on it, as the bread can burn quickly. Cool and store in an airtight container.

*Zira Nyberg Howard,
contributed by Christine Nyberg Tunstall
John and Ora Nyberg,
Washington County, 1895*

John Nyberg emigrated from Sweden. Swedish flat bread was served at all family reunions held in August on the farm until Zira died. Zira was the 7th of 10 children of John and Ora Nyberg.

— Christine Nybert Tunstall

BREAD & MUFFINS

Zetta's Banana Bread

2 eggs, beaten
1 cup sugar
½ cup shortening or butter
3 to 4 diced, ripe bananas, to make 1 cup
2½ cups flour
½ teaspoon salt
½ teaspoon baking powder
2 teaspoons baking soda
1 cup nuts
4 tablespoons milk

Mix together, put in greased baking pan, and bake in a moderate oven (325°F) for 45 minutes, or until a toothpick inserted in the middle comes out clean.

Zetta Brosnan from her mother, Bell Hager, contributed by Dyann Brosnan for Eddie Brosnan, Brosnan Ranch Jeremiah Brosnan, Morrow County, 1875

Haying on Lloyd Spires ranch, Coos County, 1940s. Debra McCormick collection

Grandma Marie's Lefse

4 cups russet potatoes, boiled and riced
¼ cup butter
½ cup half and half
1 teaspoon salt
2 teaspoons sugar
1 cup flour

Boil potatoes until soft, then rice them. While potatoes are still warm, thoroughly blend together with butter, half and half, salt, and sugar. Refrigerate overnight.

Mix 2 cups of the potato mixture with 1 cup of flour. Knead until well mixed. Roll into thin pieces on a lightly floured board. Place a piece on a griddle at high heat (approximately 500°F). Lightly brush the flour off the top of the lefse. Bake until lightly browned on the bottom, approximately 30 seconds. Use a spurdle (a lefse stick) to carefully turn the lefse. Bake an additional 15 seconds. Times and temperatures may vary.

Spread with butter; sprinkle with sugar and cinnamon. Roll up and slice into 2-inch pieces.

An ordinary pancake turner can substitute for the spurdle!

Marie Skei Simmons, contributed by Nancy Mohr, Skei-Simmons Century Farm
Ole and Karolina Skei, Clackamas County, 1905

Potatoes

The Spanish first brought potatoes to the Pacific Northwest in 1791. A major food crop, potatoes have long been a farm garden staple. Commercial production has grown with the availability of irrigation, particularly in such east-of-the-Cascades localities as Umatilla and Morrow Counties, Treasure Valley, the Klamath Basin, and Redmond. Potatoes are the state's ninth most valuable cash crop.

Apples

Motherhood and Oregon apple pies are patriotic staples. Apple seeds came to the Oregon Country in 1826, and grew into an orchard industry in the valleys of the Willamette, Hood River, and Rogue Rivers. As early as 1850, they were exported to fruit-starved California gold miners. Upstaged in recent years by more glamorous pears, apples were still harvested from some 4,200 acres in 2006, yielding a crop worth nearly $30 million.

Grandma Carrie Hobart's Apple Fritters

1 cup sifted flour
½ teaspoon salt
1½ teaspoons baking powder
1 tablespoon sugar
1 egg, beaten
½ cup milk
1 tablespoon melted fat or oil
1 cup finely chopped apples
fat for deep frying

Sift together flour, salt, baking powder, and sugar. Combine egg, milk, and fat; add to the dry ingredients all at once, stirring enough to moisten. Stir in apples. Drop by the spoonful into hot fat and cook until brown. Let cool and roll in powdered sugar.

Carrie Hobart, contributed by Roxie Hobart
Josiah Wellington Hobart,
Clackamas County, 1905

Welsh Tea Cakes

½ cup shortening
1 cup sugar
1 egg
2½ cups flour
¼ teaspoon salt
3 teaspoons baking powder
½ cup milk
½ teaspoon vanilla extract
1 cup dried currants

Thoroughly cream shortening and sugar; add egg and beat well; add flour and beat again. Add sifted dry ingredients alternately with milk and vanilla. Beat well. Add currants, beat well. Roll ⅛ inch thick on lightly floured surface. Cut with round, lightly-floured cookie cutter. Bake on greased cookie sheet in moderate oven (375°F) about 15 minutes. Remove to a cooling rack and sprinkle with sugar. Makes 3 dozen cookies.

Contributed by
Bette Davis Nelson
William X. Davies,
Clackamas County, 1886

Karen Nelson, St. Lucia Court, 1994. The Nelson family is of Swedish, Welsh and German ancestry. Bette Davis Nelson collection

My Grandfather, William X. Davis (Davies) brought this recipe from Wales when he came to Oregon in 1886 and established the Davies family farm. He was instrumental in establishing the Bryn Seion Welsh Church in Beavercreek near the farm.

These Welsh tea cakes were always made for the Gymanfra Gynu (Welsh Song Festival) the last Sunday in June. They are still served at tea time to guests who come from around the Pacific Northwest, the United States, and Wales for the festival.

— Bette Davis Nelson

BREAD & MUFFINS

Holiday French Toast

4 thick slices French or Italian bread
2 or 3 large eggs, beaten
½ cup orange juice
½ teaspoon cinnamon
½ teaspoon nutmeg
2 tablespoons honey

Combine eggs, orange juice, cinnamon, nutmeg, and honey.

Coating

1 cup crushed corn flakes or granola, ground into small pieces
½ teaspoon cinnamon
½ teaspoon nutmeg

In a small dish, mix together corn flakes or granola, cinnamon and nutmeg. Dip each bread slice in egg mixture, turning to coat both sides, then dip slices in cereal mixture. Saute coated slices of bread in a skillet with melted butter, turning only once. Serves 2 to 4.

Contributed by Debra McCormick,
great granddaughter of Lloyd Spires
Lloyd Spires, Coos County, 1890

Front row: Roy, Lloyd, Elton and Emma Spires; back row: Fred, Winnifred and Oliver Spires. Debra McCormick collection

Pies, Cobblers, Puddings & Preserves

Strawberries

In the 1880s, strawberries were widely grown for local markets in the Portland and Hood River areas. In 1910, Multnomah, Clackamas, and Hood River Counties each produced a million or more quarts of strawberries. The perishable berries reached city markets by wagon, truck, or railway express. By 1950, Oregon grew as much as a hundred million pounds of strawberries, many of them of the large, firm, and very tasty— but disease-prone— Marshall variety. Production declined in the 1980s and 1990s; by 2006, when strawberries were the state's 29th most valuable cash crop, they represented only 1 percent of the nation's production. But many said it was the tastiest 1 percent.

Mom's Rhubarb Cream Pie

Make pastry for a 10-inch single-crust pie. Line pie pan with unbaked piecrust and sprinkle with 2 tablespoons flour and 1 tablespoon sugar.

4 eggs, beaten
6 tablespoons flour
⅓ teaspoon salt
¾ teaspoon nutmeg
1 cup sour cream
3 cups sugar
6 cups chopped rhubarb

Mix together eggs, flour, salt, nutmeg, sour cream, and sugar. Add rhubarb to egg mixture and put into piecrust. Dot with butter. Bake at 425°F for 15 minutes; reduce heat to 325°F and bake another 45 minutes until set.

Contributed by Marjorie Barnes Campbell
William Barnes, Clackamas County, 1908

Mary Jane's Strawberry Preserves

Combine 4 cups strawberries (cut in half if they are large berries) with 4 cups sugar and let stand overnight. Boil 8 minutes. Add 3 tablespoons lemon juice and boil 5 more minutes. Let this stand at room temperature until cold. Pour into jars and cover with paraffin.

Note: Follow USDA guidelines for proper sterilization and canning procedures.

Contributed by Carolyn Molthan Pinto
Summers Molthan, Malheur County, 1897

CULTURAL IMAGES
Glenn & Judith Mason
8890 N.W. Ash Street
Portland, Oregon 97229

(503) 297-5892 business / home
(503) 939-6090 cell
jgmason1@juno.com

- Buying & selling fine and rare books; 19th and early 20th century paper ephemera, maps, letters & diaries; photographs and postcards; American folk art; vintage advertising; and antiques related to the American Arts & Crafts Movement.
- Providing contract services and consulting to museums, research libraries and special collections, and other cultural organizations.

We salute all the Oregon Century Farm & Ranch families for their contributions to the stability, vitality, historical development, and economic well-being of Oregon through generations of continuous perseverance, innovation, and adaptability.

PIES, COBBLERS, PUDDINGS & PRESERVES

Old Timers Cream Pie

½ cup all-purpose flour
¼ teaspoon salt
½ teaspoon ginger
¾ cup sugar
1 cup rich cream or evaporated milk
1 cup thin cream or diluted evaporated milk
cinnamon

Mix flour, salt, ginger, and sugar well. Stir into this mixture 1 cup thick cream or undiluted evaporated milk. Add this cream a little at a time to the flour and sugar mixture in order to have a smooth batter without lumps. Next stir in 1 cup of thin cream or rich milk. Stir well. Pour mixture into an unbaked pie crust. Sprinkle the top generously with cinnamon. Bake at 450º F for 10 minutes, then at 350ºF for 30 minutes. The pie will have a thin creamy appearance on top, but will thicken up as it cools.

Mollie Davenport, contributed
by granddaughter
Ann Davenport Vasconi, Kow Kamp Ranch
Benjamin and Sarah Davenport, Marion County, 1851

Bunkhouse, Hillcrest Orchard, Medford, about 1915. Hillcrest Orchard collection

Prune Conserve

1 pound raisins
4 pounds fresh prunes
juice from 4 oranges
8 cups sugar
1 pound walnut meats

Boil all ingredients except nut meats together until thick. Stir in nut meats 5 minutes before removing from heat. Pour into sterilized jars and seal while hot.

Note: Follow USDA guidelines for proper sterilization and canning procedures.

Emma Hudel Budlong, contributed by Cindi Budlong
Jacob H. and Catherine Hudel, Linn County, 1895

Rhubarb Pudding

4 cups rhubarb, cut up
3 cups bread, torn into pieces
1 cup sugar
¼ cup chopped nuts
½ teaspoon cinnamon
¼ teaspoon nutmeg

Toss ingredients together and pour ¼ cup melted butter over mixture. Put in buttered baking dish and bake at 350°F for about 40 minutes. Serve hot or cold with whipped cream.

Contributed by Roxie Hobart
Josiah Wellington Hobart, Clackamas County, 1905

Jacob Henry and Catherine Hudel settled on the property, east of Salem and north of Mill City, in 1895, and had two children. This recipe for prune conserve is from their daughter, Emma Hudel Budlong, my husband's grandmother. She made this recipe from prunes grown in the orchard planted by Jacob Henry. My mother-in-law, Bobbie Budlong, has used this recipe with prunes from the same trees to make the conserve for years, and now I make it too—it's still a family favorite.

— Cindi Budlong

PIES, COBBLERS, PUDDINGS & PRESERVES

Curried Fruit

⅓ cup butter
¾ cup brown sugar, packed
4 teaspoons curry powder

Melt butter, add sugar and curry. Pour over the following drained fruits arranged in a baking dish:

1 can pears
1 can peaches
1 can pineapple
maraschino cherries

Bake covered 1 hour at 350°F.

Ms. van der Hellen was a Parsons family acquaintance.

— Diana Gardner

Patricia von der Hellen, contributed by Diana Gardener (Mrs. Judson Parsons), Hillcrest Orchard
Reginald H. Parsons, Jackson County, 1908

Fruit packing, Hillcrest Orchard, Medford, about 1930.
Hillcrest Orchard collection

RUSTIC PEAR TART WITH
LATE-HARVEST VIOGNIER SYRUP AND CRÈME FRAICHE

The rich, fruity sweetness of our 2006 RoxyAnn Late-Harvest Viognier beautifully complements the natural sugars in roasted pears.

Crust

1½ cups all purpose flour

3 tablespoons sugar

½ teaspoon salt

10 tablespoons (1¼ stick) chilled unsalted butter, cut into pieces

1 large egg yolk

1 tablespoon late-harvest Riesling or other sweet white dessert wine

Filling

3 large ripe, but firm, Hillcrest Orchard Comice pears, peeled, cored, thinly sliced

1 tablespoon plus ½ cup sugar

1 tablespoon all purpose flour

1 cup plus 2 tablespoons late-harvest Viognier or other sweet white dessert wine

½ cup water

Crème Fraiche [store-bought or homemade]

To Make:

Crust: Blend flour, sugar, and salt in a food processor until combined. Add butter; using on/off turns, cut in until mixture resembles coarse meal. Add egg yolk and wine; using on/off turns, mix just until moist clumps form. [Note: if dough is crumbly, add teaspoons of ice water until it comes together.] Gather dough into ball; flatten into disk. Wrap in plastic and chill at least 40 minutes and up to 2 days.

Filling: Position rack in center of oven and preheat to 375°F. Roll out dough between 2 sheets of parchment paper to 12-inch round. Remove top sheet of parchment and transfer dough, with bottom parchment, to rimmed baking sheet. Place pear slices, 1 tablespoon sugar, and flour in large bowl; toss to combine. Spoon pear mixture into center of dough, leaving 1½-inch border. Using parchment as aid, fold up outer edge of dough over edge of filling. Bake until pears are tender, about 20 minutes. Meanwhile, boil 1 cup wine, ½ cup water, and remaining ½ cup sugar in medium saucepan until syrup is reduced to ½ cup, about 10 minutes. Reduce oven temperature to 325°F. Drizzle half of syrup over filling. Continue baking tart until juices are bubbling thickly, about 20 minutes. Cool. Whisk 2 tablespoons wine into remaining syrup. Cut tart into wedges. Drizzle with syrup. Serve with a dollop of crème fraiche. Serves 8.

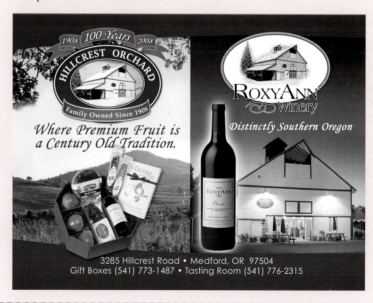

One of my fond memories from growing up on the farm was picking Himalaya berries off a large bush in the pasture, then making them into a delicious dessert served with ice cream.

The recipe works equally well as a coffee cake topped with whipped cream.

— Sylvia Olson

PIES, COBBLERS, PUDDINGS & PRESERVES

Crow's Nest Pudding

Spread 3 to 4 cups of berries (blackberries, marionberries or other caneberries) in a baking dish and lightly sprinkle with flour and sugar. Cover with batter made of:

½ cup sugar
butter the size of a walnut
1 teaspoon baking powder
1 egg
½ cup milk
flour, enough to make batter "slightly thicker than cake batter"

Bake about 40 minutes at 350°F.

Helen Dworschak, contributed by her daughter, Sylvia Olson
John Fredrich Dworschak, Clackamas County, 1893

Caramel Nut Apple Pie

1 unbaked 9-inch pie crust

Filling

1 cup sugar
¼ cup flour
½ teaspoon salt
1 tablespoon cinnamon
4 to 5 cups apples, sliced
2 tablespoons lemon juice
3 tablespoons butter, in small pieces

Topping

12 caramels
1 tablespoon cream, more as needed
½ cup toasted hazelnuts

Mix sugar, flour, salt, and cinnamon. Add apples, lemon juice, and butter. Pour into pie shell. Place a square of aluminum foil lightly over filling during baking. Bake at 425°F for 15 minutes. Reduce heat to 350°F and bake an additional 45 minutes or more, until crust is done. Remove pie from oven.

Meanwhile, microwave caramels and cream for 30 seconds. Mash caramels into the cream until mixture becomes a sauce; more heat may be needed. If needed, add additional cream by teaspoonfuls. Pour the caramel sauce on top of the hot apple pie. Then top with toasted nuts. Cool before cutting.

Charlene Peter Roberts, Peter Farm
Frederick Peter, Clackamas County, 1883

Caneberries

Blackberries, boysenberries, loganberries, raspberries, and their relatives: they are all delicious, and they have been extensively grown in the Willamette Valley since pioneer days. Canned and turned to juice, loganberries—a cross between a red raspberry and a wild blackberry—were a wildly popular crop in the early 1900s; by 2007, there were only 60 acres in production. But other caneberries were grown that year on some 10,000 acres, the crop valued at more than fifty million dollars.

PIES, COBBLERS, PUDDINGS & PRESERVES

German Apple Cobbler

Topping

2 cups flour
½ teaspoon salt
4 tablespoons baking powder
1 tablespoon sugar
⅓ cup shortening
1 egg, well beaten
½ cup milk

Sift together flour, salt, baking powder, and sugar. Cut in shortening until mixture is like coarse crumbs. Combine egg and milk and add to flour mixture, stirring just until moistened. Turn out on slightly floured surface. Pat out in a round.

Apple filling

2 cups apples, peeled and cut up
½ cup brown sugar
½ teaspoon cinnamon
½ teaspoon nutmeg

Combine ingredients in a bowl and mix thoroughly.

Grease a deep round casserole dish. Add apple filling to casserole. Cover with cobbler dough. Bake in a moderate oven (375ºF) for 30 minutes. Remove from oven and sprinkle with sugar.

Contributed by Bette Davis Nelson
William X. Davies, Clackamas County, 1886

In the Fall, apples of all the older varieties such as King, Snow, and Gravenstein, were picked and stored in a cool place on the farm for winter. Mother always made this apple cobbler for special occasions and Sunday evening supper.

— Bette Davis Nelson

Strawberry Pie

Fill a baked piecrust with fresh strawberries, each cut in half. Then combine:

2 cups strawberries, chopped
⅓ cup water
1 cup sugar
3 tablespoons cornstarch

Simmer strawberry mixture until it boils and thickens. Remove from heat and stir regularly until cool. Pour the cooked berries over the fresh berries in a pre-baked piecrust. Refrigerate until firm. To serve, top with whipped cream.

Sue Unger, Unger Enterprises
Frank Unger, Washington County, 1906

I don't know where I got this one.

— Sue Unger

Ed Castillo and Kent Bradshaw picking strawberries on Grand Island, 1946. P120:2718, courtesy Oregon State University Archives

Pears

Though they were a farm orchard staple from the 1850s, pears did not become a major commercial crop until the early 1900s, when refrigerated rail cars made it possible to ship them to distant markets. The Hood River Valley became famous for pears in the 1910s, and the Rogue River Valley in the 1930s. About a quarter of the nation's pears are grown in Oregon. The elegant pear was designated the state fruit in 2005.

Aunt Helen's Fruit Pudding

1 cup sugar
2 cups flour
1 teaspoon baking powder
½ teaspoon salt
1 cup milk
3 tablespoons butter, melted

Mix together; spread batter in greased 9x13 baking pan. Pour 1 quart fresh or frozen fruit or berries over batter. Sprinkle 1 cup sugar over berries, then pour 2 cups hot water over all. Bake at 375ºF for 30 to 45 minutes.

Especially good made with gooseberries or rhubarb. Serve with whipped cream or ice cream.

Contributed by Waynette Morin
Lewis Calvin and Laura Ellen Morin, Baker County, 1901

Pearfection

4 cups unsweetened pear sauce (pears cooked until very soft)
4 cups sugar
⅛ teaspoon salt
4 tablespoons gelatin, dissolved in 1 cup cold pineapple juice
3 cups chopped nuts
1 teaspoon lemon flavoring, or lemon juice to taste

Combine pear sauce, sugar, and salt, and cook very slowly until sauce is thick when dropped from spoon. While hot, add gelatin dissolved in juice. Mix thoroughly and add nuts and lemon. Spread in buttered pan to a depth of about ¾ inch. Let cool thoroughly and cut into bite-sized pieces. Roll each piece in powdered sugar.

> Louise Grade, contributed by Diana Gardener (Mrs. Judson Parsons),
> Hillcrest Orchard
> Reginald H. Parsons, Jackson County, 1908

Louise Grade was employed for many years by the Parsons family.

— Diana Gardner

Pear picker near Medford, 1944. HC0972, courtesy Oregon State University Archives

PIES, COBBLERS, PUDDINGS & PRESERVES

Strawberry Sun Jam

4 boxes strawberries
2 cups sugar
¼ cup lemon juice

Pour sugar over strawberries and let stand until juice develops (a couple of hours). Then add 3 more cups of sugar and let stand overnight.

Bring berries to a boil and cook 8 minutes. Add ¼ cup lemon juice and cook 2 more minutes. Put on a platter and place in the sun and let stand. If at desired thickness the next day, seal cold.

Note: Follow USDA guidelines for proper sterilization and canning procedures.

Margaret Dear Tilbury, Thomas and Dear Ranch
Richard Thomas, Douglas County, 1863

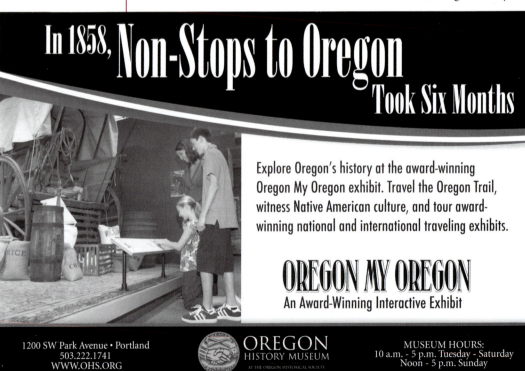

Old-Time Favorite Fruit Cobbler

Use any kind of fresh or canned fruit, to cover the bottom of an 8- or 9-inch baking dish.

1¾ cups granulated sugar, divided
3 tablespoons butter
1 teaspoon baking powder
¼ teaspoon salt
½ cup milk
1 cup sifted flour
1 tablespoon cornstarch
⅓ to ⅔ cup boiling water, depending on the juiciness of the fruit. For berries, I start with the least amount; for peaches I may use up to ⅔ cup.

Mix ¾ cup sugar with butter, baking powder, salt, milk, and flour.
Pour over fruit.

Mix 1 cup sugar with cornstarch. Sprinkle over mixture, then pour boiling water over all. Bake at 375°F for 45 minutes.

Note: if the fruit is canned with sugar or is very sweet, I use less sugar in either place sugar is called for.

Contributed by Jo Ann Tannock
George E. Zimmerman, Washington County, 1895

PIES, COBBLERS, PUDDINGS & PRESERVES

Famous Ella Allen Raisin Pudding

1½ tablespoons butter
3 cups water
1½ cups brown sugar
1 cup white sugar
1½ cups flour
1½ cups raisins, light or dark
¾ cup milk
1½ teaspoons soda
1½ teaspoons baking powder
1 teaspoon salt

Combine butter, water, and brown sugar and let come to a boil. Mix rest of ingredients together and put in a greased 9x13 pan. Pour boiled sugar water over batter, using a spoon to prevent a hole from forming. Bake at 350ºF for 25 minutes.

Ella Allen worked as a cook in the 1930s and early 1940s for Otto and Hilda Hellberg (the second generation). Ella cooked for the hay crew of 15 to 20 men, who stayed in a bunk house during the season.

— Carolyn Hellberg

Ella Allen, contributed by Carolyn Hellberg,
Hellberg Farms
Christian and Wilhelmina Hellberg,
Umatilla County, 1908

Recipe booklet from Chamberlain's Extracts, distributed by Claus Grocery, Silverton, about 1920. Author's collection

Marionberry Cobbler

1 stick butter, melted
1½ cups milk
2 cups flour
2 cups sugar
1 tablespoon baking powder
4 cups fresh or frozen marionberries
up to 2 cups sugar

Preheat oven to 350°F. Melt the butter in the bottom of a 9x13 baking pan. Mix milk, flour, 2 cups sugar, and baking powder well. Pour over melted butter. Do NOT stir. Sprinkle berries on top. Do NOT stir. Cover with up to 2 cups sugar. Do NOT stir. Bake for about 1 hour or until middle is set and edges are crispy.

Contributed by Nancy Lewis
Franklin James Lewis, Washington County, 1905

The Silverton farmhouse,
427 Grant Street, 1912

*This space contributed
by a Friend of the
Oregon Century Farm & Ranch Program*

ENGLISH BOILED PUDDING

3 cups flour
1 teaspoon cream of tartar
½ teaspoon saleratus (baking soda)
salt
sugar
cinnamon
sweet milk
shortening
apples, peeled and sliced

Make a biscuit dough with the flour, cream of tartar, baking soda, salt, and milk. Roll out in a large sheet. Toss the apples with sugar and cinnamon. Fold the dough over the apples. Moisten the dough and press together tightly; then place carefully in a clean cloth sack. Tie the sack and put it into a kettle of boiling water, and let boil until done. Remove from sack and serve warm with a sauce or thick cream. It may be varied by using different kinds of fruit.

Anne Welborn Beeson,
contributed by the Talent Historical Society.
John Beeson, Jackson County, 1853

Ad from the Pure Food Cook Book, published by the Portland Telegram, about 1907. Author's collection

Cakes, Cookies & Candy

CAKES, COOKIES & CANDY

Fluffy Banana Cake

This recipe was in my wedding present—a Sunbeam mixer—56 years ago. We still enjoy it and it uses up a lot of overripe bananas.

— Darlene Grauer

Grease and flour two 9-inch layer cake pans.

Put into the small bowl of mixer:
2 large, or 3 small, bananas, broken into chunks. Use bananas that are very ripe—too ripe for eating

Beat until mashed. Measure out 1 cup. (If you have extra banana, a little of it in a powdered sugar frosting is very good.)

Sift together:
2 cups sifted all-purpose flour
½ teaspoon baking powder
¾ teaspoon soda
½ teaspoon salt

Put into large bowl of mixer:
½ cup shortening (soft)
1½ cups sugar (you can use a little less)
2 eggs, unbeaten
1 teaspoon vanilla

Beat on high speed for 1½ minutes, scraping bowl while beating. Stop mixer and add:

¼ cup buttermilk or sour milk

Add sifted flour mixture alternately with mashed banana while beating on medium speed. Scrape bowl while beating and beat only enough to blend, about 2 minutes. Pour batter into prepared pans. Bake in moderate oven (350°F) for 30 to 35 minutes; check after 25 minutes. Cool. Fill and top with whipped cream or powdered sugar frosting.

Contributed by Darlene Grauer
Jacob and Rose Grauer, Yamhill County, 1899

Whipped Cream Cake

1 cup whipping cream
2 eggs, beaten until thick
1 cup sugar
1 teaspoon vanilla
1½ cups sifted cake flour
¼ teaspoon salt
2 teaspoons baking powder

Whip cream until it holds its shape, add eggs and whip until foamy. Add sugar, beat again, add vanilla. Sift flour, salt, and baking powder together 3 times, add to egg mixture. Bake in greased layer cake pans at 350°F for 25 to 30 minutes. Cool and spread with whipped cream or frosting.

**Contributed by Mapril Easton Combs
Robert and Emma Easton, Coos County, 1898**

This recipe was used by my mother, Mildred Neely Easton, handed down from her mother. Note that there is no shortening in the cake, as every family had a cow and chickens, and therefore plenty of milk, cream, butter and eggs.

— Mapril Easton Combs

*Spring blossoms near Medford Hillcrest Orchard, about 1920.
Hillcrest Orchard collection*

CAKES, COOKIES & CANDY

Favorite Applesauce Cake

Combine:
1½ cups sugar
⅓ cup shortening
1 egg, well beaten
1½ cups unsweetened applesauce
1½ cups raisins, currants or figs, cut up

Sift together:
2 cups flour
½ teaspoon cinnamon
½ teaspoon ginger
4 teaspoons cocoa
2 teaspoons soda

Add sifted flour and spices to sugar and applesauce mixture, beat well. Bake in a moderate (350ºF) oven until done.

Recipe from Hazel Christensen; contributed by Lyle and Cynthia Christensen
Jeppe and Lena Christensen, Yamhill County, 1902

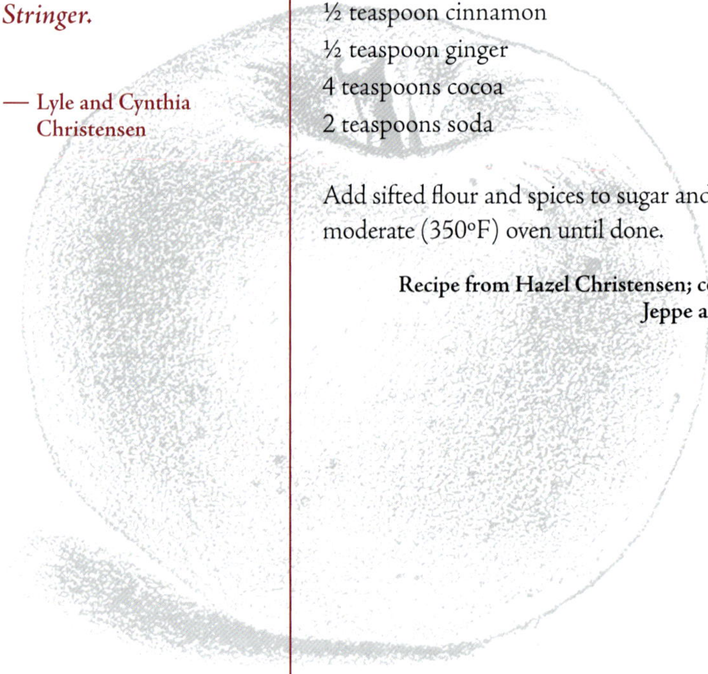

Adapted from a recipe published in a recipe book issued in 1935 by the Bellevue-Sheridan Farmers Union Auxiliary, edited by Louisa Lehmann Stringer.

— Lyle and Cynthia Christensen

Boiled Spice Cake (Depression Cake)

2 cups sugar
2 cups water
2 cups raisins
1 cup oil
1 teaspoon cloves
3 teaspoons cinnamon
1 teaspoon salt

Boil the ingredients, cool. Then add:
3 cups flour
2 teaspoons soda
walnuts (optional)

Pour into a floured 9x12 baking pan. Bake for 45 to 50 minutes at 350ºF. Makes a delicious, heavy spice cake.

Contributed by Nadine Dougherty
Robert W. and Elizabeth Dougherty,
Umatilla County, 1903

A dairy herd in clover near Dufur, ca. 1940. Ralph Gifford photo, P218:0617, courtesy Oregon State University Archives

CAKES, COOKIES & CANDY

Boiled Fruit Cake

2 cups sugar
2 cups cold water
1 tablespoon shortening
1 teaspoon salt
1 teaspoon cloves
1 teaspoon cinnamon
1½ cups walnuts
1½ cups raisins

Bring to a boil. Let cool and add 1 teaspoon baking soda and 3 cups flour. Stir together, pour into baking pan, bake at 350ºF for 1 hour.

Muriel Hafner, contributed by her daughter Sue Sutton, Hafner Farms
John Hafner, Marion County, 1907

OREGON WHEAT GROWERS LEAGUE
"The Voice of Oregon Wheat Producers Since 1926"

Oregon Wheat…
Represents more than 4,000 wheat producers and landowners across nearly 1 Million Acres

Oregon Wheat…
Makes the best cookies, cakes and pastries

Oregon Wheat…
Contributing to the Economy
Caring for the Environment
Feeding the World

OREGON WHEAT GROWERS LEAGUE
115 SE 8th St, Pendleton, Oregon 97801
541-276-7330   www.owgl.org

Old Jacksonville White Cake

⅔ cup butter
2 cups sugar
2 cups cake flour, sifted
1 teaspoon salt
1 cup milk
1 teaspoon baking soda
2 teaspoons cream of tartar
2 tablespoons flour
6 egg whites, beaten to soft peaks

Beat butter and sugar until mixture is fluffy. Then add, alternately, sifted cake flour, salt, and milk. Mix baking soda and cream of tartar with 2 tablespoons of flour. Add to batter mixture. Fold in egg whites carefully until well mixed. Grease and flour two 9-inch round cake pans. For best results, place a round of parchment paper in the bottom of each cake pan to prevent sticking. Pour batter into pans. Bake at 325ºF for 35 minutes or until a toothpick inserted comes out clean.

Hanley family recipe collection,
contributed by Southern Oregon Historical Society
Michael Hanley, Jackson County, 1857

This recipe was submitted by Alice Hanley for the *West Side Cookbook*, 1945. It is a delicious, moist white cake.

Oatmeal Chip Cookies

My mom, Margie Unger, adapted this recipe to make her own healthier version by using brown sugar and honey and increasing the amount of whole wheat. She made 500 of these well-loved cookies for a family reunion in 1998.

— Irene Unger Fish

1 cup margarine
1 cup shortening
4 cups brown sugar
4 eggs
½ cup honey
2 teaspoons baking soda
2 teaspoons salt
2¼ cups white flour
2¼ cups whole wheat flour
4 cups quick rolled oats
2 cups chopped walnuts
2 cups finely ground coconut
2 cups chocolate chips

Mix all ingredients. Best if dough is made and refrigerated for several hours before baking. Bake in a 350°F oven until done. Makes a very large batch.

Margie Unger, contributed by Irene Unger Fish
Frank Unger, Washington County, 1906

Fresh Apple Cake

4 cups sliced apples
½ cup oil
2 cups sugar
2 eggs
2 teaspoons vanilla

Stir together to mix. Add 1 cup dried cranberries, raisins, or nuts. Stir together and add:

2 cups flour
1 teaspoon salt
2 teaspoons soda
2 teaspoons cinnamon

Fold together, pour into 9x12 baking pan, and bake 1 hour at 350°F.

Gerry Kreutzer
J. J. Kreutzer, Curry County, 1902

The farm in 2007. Gerry Kreutzer collection

Grapes and wine

Grape vines were common on nineteenth-century Oregon farms and ranches, but turning grapes to wine was an activity more discussed than acted upon. Wine was produced for sale in the Rogue River Valley in the 1880s, and some wine was produced in the Umpqua and Willamette Valleys as well. Wasco County was dabbling in wine grapes in 1915, but statewide prohibition, which began in 1916, dampened things. Not until the 1960s and 1970s did vineyards have another chance in Oregon, and this time they succeeded. The 35 acres of wine grapes grown in 1970 were dwarfed by the 15,000+ acres of 2006.

Aunt Gretchen's Chewie Dewies

1 pound brown sugar
⅔ cup butter or margarine
4 eggs

Cream ingredients together, then add:

2½ cups flour
2½ teaspoons baking soda
1 teaspoon salt
1 teaspoon vanilla
1 package (6 ounces) chocolate chips
1 cup chopped nuts (optional)

Put in a greased and floured 9x13 baking pan and bake for 30 to 35 minutes at 375°F. Makes about 24 squares. Cut while still warm.

**Gretchen Cannon Anthony, contributed by Nancy Cannon
Alice Heller Cannon Coon, Wallowa County, 1884**

Recipe card, about 1925; cover, Choice Recipes, about 1930. Author's collection

Lois Hiatt Parrish's Prune Cake

1 cup sugar
½ cup butter
2 eggs
1 cup cooked prunes, chopped
2½ cups flour
1 teaspoon baking soda
2 teaspoons baking powder
1 teaspoon cloves
1 teaspoon allspice
1½ teaspoons cinnamon
pinch of salt
1 cup sour milk

Cream sugar and butter, add eggs and chopped prunes. Mix. Sift together flour, baking soda, baking powder, cloves, allspice, cinnamon, and salt. Alternately add the sour milk and the sifted dry ingredients to the sugar and prune mixture; fold together.

Turn into a well-greased 9x13 pan (or 2 pans, each 8x8) and bake at 350°F for 45 minutes. Frost when cool.

Lois Hiatt, contributed by Diane Berry
John and Elvira Teel, Umatilla County, 1893

We used sea foam frosting or brown sugar frosting.

Lois Hiatt was my maternal great great aunt. The recipe originally came from Princess Thomson and Della Bartholomew, members of an old Echo family that has farmed on Butter Creek west of Echo for over a century. It has become a favorite of Echo bakers and my family.

— Diane Berry

Harvesting on the Bartholomew farm on Butter Creek, 1916. Diane Berry collection

CAKES, COOKIES & CANDY

Maple Bars

1 cake yeast
1 pint warm milk
½ cup sugar
1 teaspoon salt
¼ cup butter, softened
5 to 6 cups flour, or enough to make a stiff dough

Dissolve the yeast in the warm milk; stir in sugar, salt, and butter. Then stir in enough flour to make a stiff dough. Knead until dough is smooth. Shape into rolls, each a little larger than your third finger and about 5 inches long. Let it rise like bread. Fry in deep fat fryer; cool and frost.

Maple Icing

½ cup brown sugar
6 tablespoons cream
½ teaspoon maple flavoring

Let boil until creamy, stirring constantly. Add ½ teaspoon maple flavoring, and enough powdered sugar to make a nice icing. Add to maple bars and enjoy!

Contributed by Trena Gray
Bruno F. Medler, Sherman County, 1901

Cover of promotional pamphlet, issued by Sunset Magazine Homeseekers' Bureau, Sherman County Development League, Oregon Railway & Navigation Co., and Southern Pacific Co., 1910. Cultural Images collection

Fresh Raspberry Cake

Sift together:
2 cups flour
1½ teaspoons baking powder
½ teaspoon soda
1 teaspoon salt
1 teaspoon cinnamon

Blend together, creaming well:
½ cup shortening
1¼ cups sugar
add 3 eggs, one at a time, and beat for 1 minute

Combine:
¾ cup buttermilk
1 teaspoon vanilla

Add buttermilk mixture alternately with dry ingredients to creamed mixture, beginning and ending with dry ingredients. Blend thoroughly after each addition (with electric mixer, use low speed). Fold in 1 to 2 cups fresh raspberries. Pour into two well-greased and lightly floured 8-inch round layer pans and bake at 350°F for 30 to 40 minutes. You can also bake in a 9x13 inch pan. This is good topped with whipped cream and fresh raspberries. I think marionberries might be used in place of the raspberries.

Pink Raspberry Frosting

Cream ⅓ cup butter and ½ teaspoon salt. Blend in 3 cups sifted powdered sugar alternately with 2 tablespoons raspberries. Add 2 to 3 tablespoons hot cream and 1 teaspoon vanilla. Mix thoroughly.

Contributed by Annell Carlson
Gust and Mathilda Carlson, Multnomah County, 1905

My daughter entered this in 4-H at the Oregon State Fair. She used the round pans and frosted the cake with pink raspberry frosting. You can add some fresh raspberries as garnish.

My sister sent this cake to our brother when he was in Vietnam during the war. She used boysenberries instead of the raspberries. They were a little moldy when he received the cake, but he loved receiving berries from home.

— Annell Carlson

Great Grandma Smith's Sugar Cookies

1 cup sugar
1 cup shortening
2 eggs, slightly beaten and placed in measuring cup; fill to 1 cup mark with cream
6 teaspoons baking powder
pinch of salt
1 teaspoon vanilla
3 cups flour, or enough to make a stiff dough

Mix together. Roll out and cut with cookie cutters and decorate. Bake at 350ºF for 8 to 10 minutes. Do not brown.

Great grandma always topped these cookies with a walnut half.

— Betty Jo Smith

Contributed by Betty Jo Smith
Robert L. Smith, Linn County, 1890

Vernon's Favorite Glazed Hazelnuts

2 cups roasted whole Oregon hazelnuts
1 cup roasted Oregon hazelnuts, finely ground
1 cup sugar
⅓ cup milk
1 teaspoon rum extract
1 teaspoon vanilla extract

Combine the sugar and milk in a saucepan and cook to a soft ball stage, without stirring, 236ºF. Remove from heat, add extracts and whole nuts. Stir until mixture coats nutmeats. Turn into a bowl containing the finely ground hazelnuts. Quickly coat as you separate the nuts. Turn onto wax paper and let cool.

Nancy Mohr, Skei-Simmons Century Farm
Ole and Karolina Skei, Clackamas County, 1905

Sophisticated, with a reputation for exotic taste — that's us in a nutshell.

OREGON Hazelnuts. Two magical words that instantly add toasted flavor and flair to entrées, desserts, salads, sauces, and more. Long favored by chefs for their exotic taste and versatility in everything from pesto to pies, these gourmet gems develop their deeply distinctive flavor from the rich volcanic and glacial soil of the breathtaking Willamette Valley. Here, where Oregon Hazelnut's flavor is born, farmers are connected to the land by five generations of growers before them. That's why they take such pride in being caretakers of the crops. It's no wonder 99% of all domestic hazelnuts come from Oregon…our local flavor is extremely deep-rooted. *Ask for Oregon Hazelnuts by name.*

Oregon
HAZELNUTS
Indulgence in a Nutshell

www.OREGONHAZELNUTS.org

CAKES, COOKIES & CANDY

Cherries

The Pacific Northwest produces more than half the nation's cherries, especially the sweet ones. The Bing, Lambert, and Rainier varieties were all developed here, and Salem was a major cherry-raising center by 1890, when the Salem Canning Company was shipping them across the country. Salem became known as the Cherry City in 1907. Much of the cherry growing has shifted to orchards in Wasco and Hood River Counties in recent decades. Still, the city buses in Salem are called Cherriots.

Hood River Brandied Cherries

6 pounds Hood River Bing cherries (or any variety of dark, sweet cherry)
1½ cups sugar
1⅓ cups water
2 tablespoons lemon juice
1½ cups Hood River Monarch brand brandy

Wash, stem, and pit cherries. Prepare by sterilizing 6 pint jars and lids for boiling water bath.

Combine sugar, water, and lemon juice in a saucepan. Boil to dissolve sugar.

In hot jars, pour ¼ cup hot syrup over cherries that are tightly packed to within ½" of top, add ¼ cup brandy and more syrup if necessary to cover cherries.

Shake jars, releasing air bubbles, wipe jar rims, and close jars tightly with lid. Process in boiling water for 20 minutes. Follow manufacturer's directions for safe canning techniques.

Ways to Use Cherries

Drain cherries and add 2 teaspoon cornstarch to reserved syrup. Stir, bring to a boil until thickened. Reheat cherries in sauce and serve.

To flame: pour warm cherries and syrup in shallow skillet or chafing dish. Pour 2 tablespoons of warmed brandy on cherries. Light with match, stir until flame is gone, and spoon over cake or ice cream.

Contributed by Sydney Blaine
Avalon Orchards/Sydney Babson and Rea Babson, Hood River County, 1908

Lemon Bars

2 sticks butter
½ cup powdered sugar
2 cups all-purpose flour
4 eggs, well beaten
½ teaspoon salt
2 cups sugar
8 tablespoons lemon juice
½ tablespoon grated lemon rind
4 tablespoons flour
1 tablespoon baking powder

Cream first three ingredients together and spread evenly in an ungreased jelly roll pan. Bake for 15 minutes at 350°F until lightly brown. Beat eggs, mix with remaining ingredients, pour over baked pastry. Bake additional 30 minutes at 325°F. Sprinkle with powdered sugar. Cool for 15 minutes, then cut into bars. Store in refrigerator.

Doris Reeves, contributed by Carol Root Seeber
Amos Root, Wasco County, 1878

This recipe was given to me by Doris Reeves, a dear friend and neighbor, at my bridal shower. It has become a family favorite over the years.

— Carol Root Seeber

FIND FARM AND RANCH HISTORY AT YOUR LOCAL MUSEUM.
WWW.OREGONMUSEUMS.ORG

OREGON MUSEUMS ASSOCIATION
P.O. BOX 1718 PORTLAND OR 97208
INFO@OREGONMUSEUMS.ORG

CAKES, COOKIES & CANDY

Ginger Snaps

two cups of cooking Molasses
one half cup of butter
three rounded teaspoons of soda
two teaspoonfuls of ginger

Mix all together. Set on the stove and boil one minute. Take off and stir in all the flour you can while hot. Roll thin and bake in a quick oven.

Contributed by Jim Cook
and Richard Cook
J. P. Cook,
Clackamas County, 1900

This recipe was found in an old family ledger that dates back to the early 1900s. I have copied this ginger snap recipe exactly as written.

— Jim Cook

A recipe for a jelly roll cake written in an 1880 day book of Boston Mills near Shedd. Now Thompson's Mills State Heritage Site, the water-powered grain mills date from 1858. Recycling paper is an ancient practice. Collection of Oregon Parks & Recreation Department, courtesy Doug Crispin

Grandma's Oatmeal Cookies

2 cups sugar
1 cup butter
2 eggs, beaten
1 teaspoon vanilla
1¼ cups ground raisins or Oregon currants (optional)
1 teaspoon baking soda
⅛ teaspoon salt
2 cups oatmeal (regular)
2½ cups flour

Cream sugar and butter. Stir in beaten eggs and vanilla, then raisins. Add soda and salt to oatmeal and flour. Mix altogether. Take small balls of dough and flatten on pan. Bake on well-greased cookie sheet, 10 to 15 minutes at 350°F.

Sarah Ethel Baker Cook (or perhaps her mother, Olive Mary Simpson Baker), contributed by Susan Cook Matherly J. P. Cook, Clackamas County, 1900

In the 1950s version, my mom, Lois McCart Cook, would add chocolate chips and nuts. In the 2000s version, my family enjoys the dough rolled in nuts, sesame seeds, or coconut before flattening and baking. I made and sent these cookies to my great uncle, Ethel's youngest brother William Kenneth Baker as one of his surprises for his 90th birthday. … He was very emotional. I told him I had sent them because they were made from his sister's recipe. His response was ohhhhh, I remember them and think it may have been my Mother's recipe.

The Hugh Baker farm was not far from the Cook farm. It was always said of my Grandmother, "she was born a Baker, married a Cook, and never got out of the kitchen."

— Lois McCart Cook

Sarah Ethel (Baker) Cook in her kitchen. Rick Cook collection

CAKES, COOKIES & CANDY

Blueberry Oatmeal Cookies

½ cup butter or margarine
1 cup dark brown sugar, packed
¾ cup granulated sugar
2 eggs
2¼ cups all-purpose flour
2 teaspoons baking powder
½ teaspoon baking soda
½ teaspoon salt
½ teaspoon cinnamon
½ teaspoon nutmeg
1 cup quick-cooking rolled oats
1 cup chopped nuts
1 cup blueberries

Cream butter until fluffy. Stir in sugars. Beat in eggs. Sift together flour, baking powder, soda, salt, cinnamon, and nutmeg, and add to creamed mixture with oats and nuts. Fold in blueberries. Push dough from heaping teaspoon onto greased cookie sheet. Bake in preheated hot over, 400°F, 10 to 12 minutes or until cookies are light brown. Makes about 36 cookies.

Contributed by Dr. William H. MacFarlane
Mark A. Hattan, Clackamas County, 1847

Ad leaflet from about 1905. Author's collection

Dream Puffs

1 cup margarine or butter
2½ cups flour
⅓ cup water
1 tablespoon vinegar

Mix like pie dough. Roll out 1/8 inch thick and cut in 2-inch circles. Bake at 350°F for 15 to 30 minutes, or until brown.

Filling

2 tablespoons milk or cream
3 cups powdered sugar
½ cup margarine or butter
½ teaspoon vanilla

Beat until fluffy. Put between two rounds. Color green or red for holidays.

Contributed by Mary Ann Scott
John King, Marion County, 1849

Vin Casteel made [these] at Victor Point School, 1967

— Mary Ann Scott

When the air turned crisp in the fall we would walk across a field behind the house to my great-uncle's walnut trees, and gather burlap bags of the pungent nuts. This triggered a season of my mother and grandmother baking, using the nuts in everything from the nut wafer cookies to "prune conserve."

— Kimberly Dunn

Nut Wafer Cookies

5 cups pastry flour
1 teaspoon salt
2 teaspoons soda
1 teaspoon cinnamon or other spices
1½ cups melted shortening
1 cup brown sugar
1 cup white sugar
3 eggs, well beaten
1 cup chopped nuts (walnuts or other nuts)

Sift flour twice with salt, soda, and cinnamon. Cream shortening with sugar. Add eggs, slowly mix thoroughly, and add nuts, and then the dry ingredients. Mix together.

Shape into rolls, 3″ in diameter. Put in pans greased with shortening; keep in refrigerator overnight. Slice when ready to bake in a hot oven, 425°F. Makes 75 cookies.

Contributed by Kimberly Dunn
Sebastian and Mary Brutscher, Yamhill County, 1850

Irene's Angel Food Cake Icing

1 cup cream
1 cup sugar
7 egg yolks
1½ teaspoon vanilla

Mix cream, sugar, and egg yolks. Cook in a heavy saucepan over medium heat until mixture comes to a full boil. Add vanilla. Cool in refrigerator. Ice an angel food cake and keep refrigerated until served.

Irene Speckhart from her stepmother, Irene Speckhart; contributed by Joanne (Speckhart) Lowry-Parsons, Speckhart Farms John Speckhart, Union County, 1904

Recipe was likely developed during the 1930s using eggs from their chickens and cream from milking their cow. The icing has been on birthday cakes in our family for at least 70 years!

— Joanne (Speckhart) Lowry-Parsons

SPICED PEARS.
Halfs 7 lb. medium winter pears. Peel and core.
Place in solution of 3 quarts water plus 3 TBS. Heinz
Distilled white vinegar to prevent browning.
Combine 2 cups sugar,
3/4 cup light corn syrup
1 cup heinz Distilled W Vinegar
1 cup water
2 small pieces whole ginger
1 small Cinnamon stick broken
1½ tsp whole cloves.
Heat to boiling, covered. Add pears Cover, Boil 3
to 5 min. Fill hot sterilized jars with pears,
Fill with boiling liquid to 1" from top
seal as directed for type of lid used.
Submerge in boiling water bath.
Process 15 min yields 6 pts.

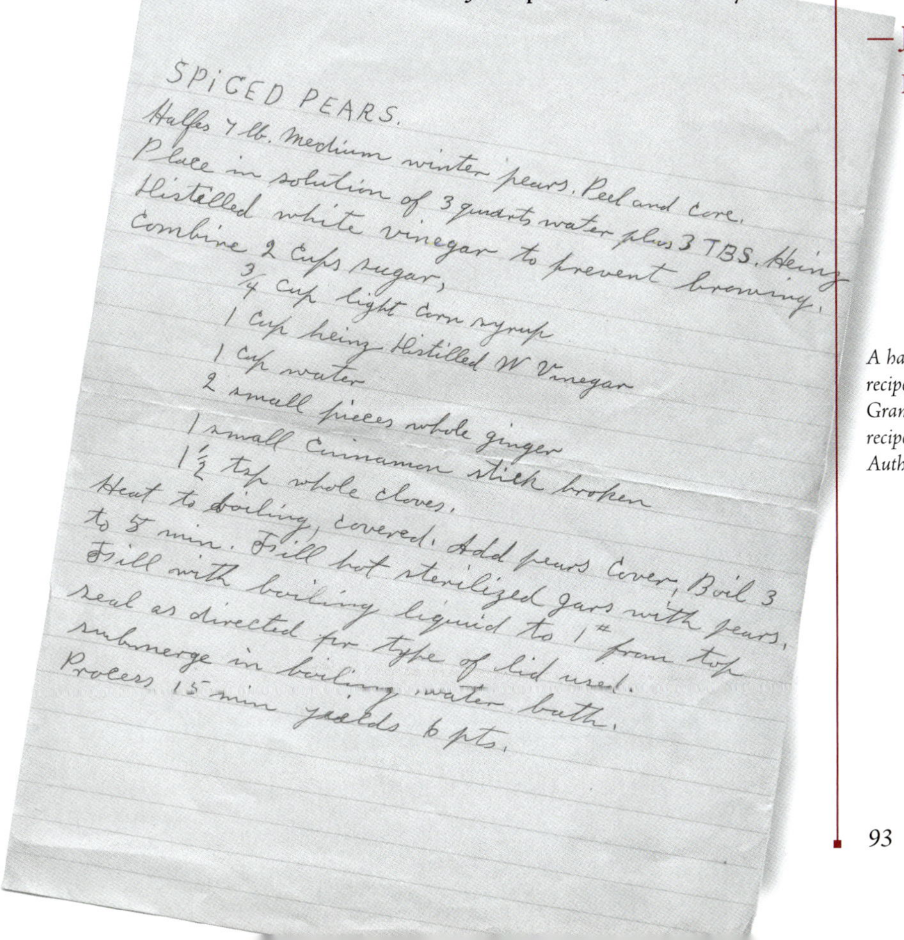

A handwritten recipe found in Grandma Dora's recipe scrapbook. Author's collection

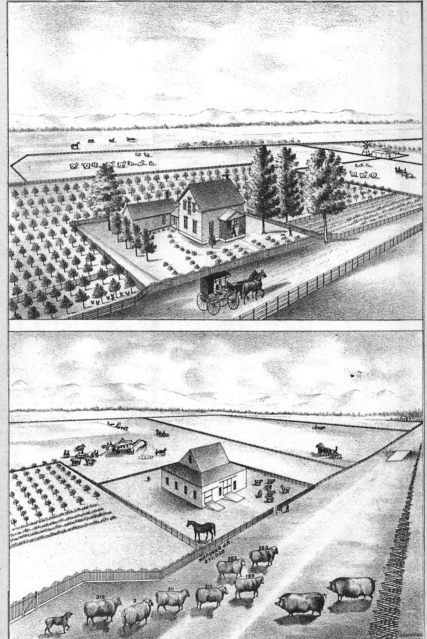

From the Historical Atlas Map of Marion and Linn Counties, Oregon. San Francisco: Edgar Williams & Co., 1878

Household Tips & Miscellany

HOUSEHOLD TIPS & MISCELLANY

All-Purpose Spray Cleaner

In a 1-quart spray bottle, combine:

⅛ cup regular or sudsy ammonia
½ cup rubbing alcohol
Top off bottle with water

I use this for EVERY-thing! Glass, furniture, bathrooms, etc.

— Paula B. Bangs

Paula B. Bangs, Bangs Family Farm
Frederick and Daisy Bangs, Lane County, 1903

Peanut Butter Playdough

2 cups peanut butter
½ cup honey
1 cup powdered milk

Mix all ingredients well. Store in Ziplock bag in fridge if any left. Completely edible, just be sure to wash hands well, before and after playing with it.

Contributed by Shirley Heater
Lorenzo D. Heater, Marion County, 1852

Dry Roasted Hazelnuts

I put the nuts in a baking pan with sides (of course!) in a single layer, and roast them at 325°F for however long it takes. The hotter the oven, the sooner they burn. Every 5 minutes, I take one out on a spoon and let it cool for a minute, then taste it. And then set the timer for another 5 minutes. Of course, the first three tastes are never done, but they give me a baseline to judge how done they are getting. It can take about 20 minutes or more, depending on how dry the nuts are and how hot the oven is.

When I take the nuts out of the oven I let them sit for 5 minutes, and then I pinch each nut to get the brown skin to crack off. They are really hot, so I work fast and don't spend time on each nut, just try to hit each one—whatever comes off is good enough for now. Then I let them cool completely, and as I transfer them to a Ziploc bag, I try to get more of the skin to come off; about 20 percent never comes off. When I want salted nuts, I put some roasted nuts in a Ziploc bag, add oil and salt, and shake it up.

Charlene Peter Roberts, Peter Farm
Frederick Peter, Clackamas County, 1883

Two college students picking filberts (hazelnuts) in Benton County, about 1945. P120:2575, courtesy Oregon State University Archives

Hazelnuts

Commercial production of hazelnuts in Oregon began in the 1890s, and they were widely planted throughout the Willamette Valley in the early twentieth century. Their popularity declined after World War II, but a resurgence of interest boosted production in the 1980s. Oregon produces nearly all of the nation's crop; in 2006, some 28,200 acres of hazelnuts were harvested, valued at more than $46 million. Once only a dessert treat in cookies and candies, hazelnuts now garnish green salads and (crushed, of course) add a crunchy crust to fish fillets.

HOUSEHOLD TIPS & MISCELLANY

Christmas Tree Crops

While the Douglas-fir has recently been put to use to flavor a liqueur (Clear Creek Distillery makes such a brandy), the tree is better known as a timber product than an agricultural one. But Christmas trees are viewed as a crop, and a profitable one in Oregon. Since 1950, the state has become a huge exporter of seasonal greenery, and Christmas trees were Oregon's 8th-largest cash crop in 2006.

To Catch Wild Ducks

To catch wild ducks alive, soak wheat in strong alcohol and scatter where they eat and take them when they are drunk.

Hint from an 1860s cookbook, contributed by Nancy Mohr,
Skei-Simmons Century Farm
Ole and Karolina Skei, Clackamas County, 1905

To Shell Large Batch of Fresh Peas

Pour boiling water over pea pods and let stand a couple of minutes or so. Drain when ready. You can almost squeeze peas out of their pods. Easiest with huge batches to do, in a cleaned, scoured, stopped-up sink. It keeps your fingers from getting sore!

Paula B. Bangs, Bangs Family Farm
Frederick and Daisy Bangs, Lane County, 1903

Homemade Lye Soap

1 can lye
2½ pints water
4 tablespoons borax
6 pints clean lard

Pour water into gallon jar or large stainless steel ONLY pot. (I use my largest stainless steel bowl.) Add lye carefully, and borax. Stir with clean, de-barked stick or large wooden spoon. It will heat up. Cool to lukewarm. Melt fat, and cool it to lukewarm too. Add fat slowly to lye mixture, stirring gently and thoroughly until it is the consistency of (thin) honey.

Pour into molds. You can use wax paper-lined Pyrex (NO metal! Remember this!), or clean, used milk cartons. Pour only as deep as the thickness of soap you want, about 1 to 1½ inches. Cut after 24 hours. Keep at room temperature for 3 days. You can wrap individually, then let ripen 3 weeks before using. The longer this soap ripens, the better it gets.

Paula B. Bangs, Bangs Family Farm
Frederick and Daisy Bangs, Lane County, 1903

I've used this for almost 40 years—although not much now that our kids are all raised and we don't raise hogs much.

— Paula B. Bangs

A farmhouse kitchen of the 1910s.
Cultural Images collection

Oregon's Agricultural History

The careful stewardship of the land that produces our food is an ancient human practice. For many hundreds of years, in what is today the state of Oregon, Indians engaged not only in harvesting bountiful foods such as salmon, wapato, and elk, but also in practices that encouraged the production or helped in the harvest of other foods. Periodic burning, for example, improved forage grasslands and aided in the harvest of tarweed seeds in the Willamette Valley.

The arrival of Euro-American settlers in the region early in the nineteenth century brought the introduction of many new animal and plant species. At Fort Vancouver, established near present-day Vancouver, Washington, in 1825, the Hudson's Bay Company planted orchards and wheat fields. Dairy cattle were pastured on nearby Sauvie Island. Retired Hudson's Bay Company fur trappers, a number of them of French-Canadian origin, settled in the Willamette Valley beginning in the 1830s on what is now known as French Prairie.

The richness of the Willamette Valley soil became known in the United States, and Americans intent on farming came to Oregon by the hundreds in the 1840s—despite the fact that it was not firmly American territory until 1846. These were the "Eden seekers" described by historian Malcolm Clark, seeking land for self-sustaining farming. The rapid influx of settlers brought Oregon to the status of a U. S. territory in 1853, and to statehood in 1859.

While the Willamette Valley was the first area to attract agricultural settlement, by the 1850s family farmers and ranchers were taking up land claims in the valleys of the Rogue and Umpqua Rivers, and by the 1860s and 1870s to the east of the Cascade Range in present-day Wasco and Union Counties. The late nineteenth century saw the development of livestock ranches in southeastern

Klamath and Lake Counties, and sheep and wheat ranches in the Columbia Plateau counties such as Sherman and Gilliam.

The twentieth century brought major changes to agriculture: steam- and then gasoline-powered machinery, improved transportation such as refrigerated rail cars and farm-to-market roads, and new crops such as hazelnuts. Irrigation projects opened up new agricultural possibilities in Central Oregon, the Klamath Basin, Treasure Valley, and the Umatilla area: potatoes, melons, sugar beets, onions, and alfalfa. Fruit production blossomed, and wheat ranching on the Columbia Plateau reached high levels.

Plant nurseries were an early and important part of Oregon agriculture; since World War II, nursery crops have become the single largest segment of the industry. But among Oregon's distinctive agricultural attributes has been the wide diversity of its crops, as well as the continued domination of family-owned farms and ranches in a nation that is increasingly characterized by corporate and industrial-type operations.

The list of Oregon agricultural products is long and varied. Some once-prominent crops have come and gone—or nearly so: flax, plums and prunes, hops, and walnuts, for example. Crops once produced only for local consumption have found new and often distant markets. Other crops have come and stayed, encouraged by the water from new irrigation projects or the new and rising popularity of an old product, such as wine. The changes have been prompted by research and development, particularly that which came out of the work of the land-grant college, today's Oregon State University and its statewide Extension Service. The families of Oregon's Century Farms & Ranches have also adjusted and adapted, and those traits—along with persistence and dedication—characterize their long-term success.

Nursery Crops

The nursery business in Oregon can be traced back to brothers Seth Lewelling and Henderson Luelling (they could not agree on how to spell the name), who brought seedlings across the plains in the 1840s. The Willamette Valley became a prime nursery region by 1900, serving a national market. Trees and shrubs have been supplemented by such crops as iris bulbs and dahlia tubers. Nurseries were a billion-dollar-a-year business in Oregon by 2006.

History of Oregon Century Farm & Ranch Program

On September 2, 1958, the Oregon State Fair hosted a ceremony that honored 354 Oregon farming families. Each family had been continuously engaged in farming, on the same land, for a hundred years or more, and they represented the descendants of 232 pioneering farm families. At the ceremony, Governor Robert D. Holmes paid tribute to the value of Oregon's agricultural heritage, and presented each of the recipients with a handsome certificate. These certificates and distinctive roadside signs have been hallmarks of the program ever since.

The Oregon Century Farm program, as it was first called, was initiated that year by the Oregon Department of Agriculture under Robert J. Steward, in collaboration with the Oregon Historical Society and its new and dynamic director, Thomas Vaughan. The purpose was to celebrate the importance of agriculture in Oregon's history, and to help commemorate the centennial of Oregon statehood, which would occur on February 14, 1959. The program was patterned after one established by the New York Agricultural Society in 1937, called the Order of Century Farms. A similar program began in Pennsylvania in 1948, and a number of other states followed. On August 30, 2008, a ceremony at the Oregon State Fair marked the fiftieth anniversary of what is now the Oregon Century Farm & Ranch Program.

When the program began in 1958, farms in fifteen Oregon counties were on the list of honorees. Only three of the farms were east of the Cascade Mountains, and all of those were in Wasco County. There were sixty-seven recipients in Marion County, fifty-five in Linn, forty-six in Yamhill; there was one each in Clatsop and Josephine Counties. To qualify for the award, applicants were required to fill out a short form attesting to the direct family descent of land ownership and its continued agricultural use. The document had to be certified by a judge of the county court—today's equivalent is a member of the county board of commissioners. Special prizes were given to those who represented the oldest farm—that of the James H. Moisan family, which settled near present-day Brooks in 1842—and the oldest farmer, Mrs. Amos Wilkins of Lane County, age 97. It took nearly two hours for the governor to greet and congratulate each family!

At the Oregon Centennial celebration in the summer of 1959, another forty-four families were inducted into the ranks. Thereafter, through 1995, the ceremonies were held at the State Fair every five years, with, of course, exceptions: inductions were made in 1973 to mark the centennial of the Oregon Pioneer Association; in 1974, when "agriculture" was the theme of the Oregon State Fair, and in 1976, the year of the national bicentennial. With all that extra activity, the ceremonies for 1975 were annulled.

Presentations are now made annually, and the total number of designated Century Farms and Ranches now exceeds 1,000. By 2008, there were Century Farms and Ranches in all but one Oregon county. There were 252 ranches and farms east of the Cascade Mountains, a marked contrast with the three that were designated in 1958. In the Willamette Valley, Yamhill, Clackamas, and Washington Counties each had enrolled more than eighty Century Farms and Ranches by 2004.

The original partners have continued to contribute to the success of the program, and have been bolstered by new supporters. For more than four decades, the Oregon Historical Society housed the program, and the application files and other program records continue to be housed in the Society's research library. Since 2000, the program has been a designated activity of the Oregon

Oregon State Fair premium award list, 1886. Cultural Images collection

Agricultural Education Foundation (OAEF), the education arm of the Oregon Farm Bureau. The Oregon Department of Parks and Recreation also lends support to the program. Contributions also come from a variety of agriculture-related firms and agencies, including a number of county farm bureaus, the Oregon Hazelnut Marketing Board, Roth's Fresh Markets, Capital Press, Tillamook County Creamery Association, and the Oregon Wheat Growers League.

On February 14, 2008, the Oregon state senate adopted a resolution to "recognize and honor the important present and future role in this state played by Oregon families that continuously own and operate the same Oregon farm or ranch for 150 or more years." The same day, fourteen families received a certificate as a Sesquicentennial Farm or Ranch—families that had continued to work their land at least another fifty years beyond the centennial mark.

Much has changed in the past 150 years of Oregon agriculture: crops, equipment, transportation, markets. In much of the nation, the family-run farm or ranch is today a rarity, supplanted by a corporate operation geared to monocrop agriculture. In Oregon, family-run operations still dominate the field, and the state's awareness of the necessity for sustained and sustainable agriculture suggests continued support for them. We salute the thousands of Oregonians who are members of families that have engaged in farming in ranching here for more than a century.

Roster of Oregon Century Farms & Ranches Since 1958

This roster lists the initial farms and ranches that have been designated since the Oregon Century Farm & Ranch Program was inaugurated in 1958. The roster was compiled from the records of the Program, held at the research library of the Oregon Historical Society in Portland. The roster is based on the original application files; however, the information required for an application has changed over the years, and by the very nature of its collection may be incomplete, unverifiable, or mistaken. Members of Century Farm & Ranch Program families are invited to submit additional information to their files to make them more complete, better documented, and more accurate.

The roster is arranged by county, and then alphabetically by surname. Spousal names are often included, but they were not always easily available. The year of the initial farm or ranch activity is also included. Keep in mind that any one initial farm or ranch may over time have devolved into two or three or more properties, each of which incorporates some of the original land and each of which is still in family-held agricultural use. As a result, the number of farms and ranches on this list is smaller than the actual number of farms and ranches that have been given the "Century" designation since 1958.

A 4-H member displays 12-foot stalks of Gold King corn, near Junction City, 1933. P120:7095, courtesy Oregon State University Archives

In compiling this version, the roster was compared with other lists prepared by the Oregon Historical Society or published in newspapers and magazines. It was not possible to satisfactorily reconcile all the discrepancies between these information sources. Some family names had more than one spelling. Sometimes it was not clear if a name referred to a sibling or a spouse. Sometimes a farm or ranch extended across a county boundary, and we chose, for simplicity's sake, to assign it to a single county. Sometimes the date of the farm or ranch founding was in doubt, and we made an executive decision to choose a year, rather than to be indefinite.

ROSTER OF OREGON CENTURY FARMS & RANCHES SINCE 1958

Baker County

Anderson, Frank O.	1883
Boyer, Thomas	1882
Brown, William	1867
Chandler, George	1864
Davis, John S.	1872
Estes, Lorena Barbara	1904
Fisher, Matthew K.	1879
Greener, Andrew P.	1877
Hill, Doc	1887
Holcomb, Candace E.	1880
Izatt, Alexander S.	1904
Koopman, Fritz	1884
Loennig, Arnst	1873
Maxwell, J. O.	1880
McEnroe, James Michael	1872
McNutt, James	1883
Morin, Lewis Calvin and Laura Ellen Phillips	1901
Murray, James Bruce	1881
Osborn, Stephen	1862
Parker, Jonathan H.	1872
Perkins, E. P.	1874
Poulson, Peter	1871
Trimble, John	1884
Troy, John	1902
Wendt, Henry	1872
Wilson, Sebrid	1885

Benton County

Armstrong, George	1873
Barclay, James E.	1851
Belknap, Ransom A.	1847
Bethers, George W.	1858
Buchanan, John A.	1885
Buckingham, Herman C.	1850
Bush, Howard Lee	1892
Currier, J. M.	1850
Elliott, William H.	1858
Harris, John	1853
Hayden, Thomas C.	1854
Henderson, Perman	1858
Herron, Robert	1853
Horning, Frederick August	1850
Humphrey, George	1869
Knotts, William and Silva	1848
Locke, A. N.	1857
Noble, Henry and Mercy	1848
Norton, Lucius C. and Hopestill	1846
Rickard, Andrew	1860
Rickard, John	1852
Schmidt, P. J. and Dorthea	1903
Schultz, George	1858
Skeels, Chester	1875
Starr, Susan A. and Wesley	1851
Sylvester, Mary	1849

Clackamas County

Aden, John	1876
Albright, Daniel	1857
Andersen, Peder Johan	1885
Anderson, Andrew	1883
Anderson, Fred	1900
Armstrong, George C.	1884
Athey, Mathew	1875
Baker, Endymian and Sarah Jane	1852
Barnes, William	1908
Boring, William H.	1876
Brackett, Henderson H.	1865
Bruck, John J.	1906
Bruck, Peter Joseph	1905
Burbage, Ezekial	1857
Callahan, Clifton	1852
Carman, Waters and Lucretia	1853
Clarke, Irving Lewis	1876
Cook, J. P.	1900

Promotional brochure issued by Corvallis Commercial Club, Sunset Homeseekers' Bureau, and Southern Pacific Co., 1909. Cultural Images collection

Crisell, William A.	1868
Daniels, Joseph Lehi	1905
Daniels, Thomas	1884
Daugherty, Giles	1864
Davies, William X.	1886
Davis, John	1888
Deininger, John F.	1896
Drescher, John	1892
Dworschak, John Fredrich	1893
Forman, George	1882
Gerber, Jacob, Jr., and Aurelia	1883
Glover, John	1852
Gribble, Andrew E.	1847
Gribble, John	1846
Guttridge, Christopher Henney	1874
Harms, John	1872
Hattan, Mark A.	1847
Heater, Peter	1877
Hobart, Josiah Wellington	1905
Jackson, Andrew and Mary	1852
Jackson, George W.	1849
James, Thomas	1855
Johnson, Andrew	1887
Kirchem, Mathias and Elizabeth	1869
Klingler, John Henry	1851
Koellermeier, August	1879
Koellermeier, Friedrich and Sophia	1876
Kraft, Henry	1904
Kraxberger, John and Rosina	1892
Kruse, John and Iantha	1852
Kruse, John and Louisa	1872
Kruse, Otto	1863
Lingelbach, Valentine	1883
Mark, Alexander K. and Sarah Jane	1847
Marquam, Alfred	1846
Marrs, Lafayette	1864
Miley, Jacob	1882
Morris, David C.	1864
Moshberger, John and Frederick	1853
Mostul, Thomas A. and Elizabeth	1904
Mulvany, N. R.	1872
Olsen, John, and August Olsen	1905
Palmateer, Garret	1853
Palmateer, John W.	1853
Peter, Frederick	1883
Peters, August and Louisa	1875
Ringo, Hulda and Harbert C.	1865
Scheer, George	1876
Schneider, John E.	1887
Schuttel, John and Rosa	1888
Skei, Ole and Karolina	1905
Smith, Washington G.	1878
Sprague, Alfred	1855
Sturm, William (Wilhelm)	1885
Suter, Eli C. and James A.	1882
Trullinger, Gabriel and Sarah	1852
Tucker, Branch	1853
Vaughan, William Hatchette	1844
Vonderahe, C. F.	1857
Voss, Joseph and Elizabeth	1850
Weddeler, Christoph and Johanne	1881
Wettlaufer, William Henry	1906
Wright, Harrison	1858
Yergen, Augustus	1855

Clatsop County

Anderson, Charles E.	1889
Cahill, Thomas	1876
Henningsen, Thor and Kristine	1902
Morrison, Robert	1845
Young, Johanna and Andrew	1885

Columbia County

Bennett, Joseph Hall	1881

Johnson, Louis 1888
Keasey, Eden W. 1896
Larson, C. J. 1907
Morten, Erik 1889

Coos County

Breuer, Samuel 1888
Catching, James Centers 1872
Crawford, Sam 1856
Davenport, Joseph A. 1900
Easton, Robert and Emma 1898
Flam, John 1872
Hamblock, John 1857
Harmon, L. L. 1873
Hayes, James D. 1889
Heller, Louis 1869
Hermann, Washington P. 1873
Hoffman, Abraham 1854
Mast, William P. 1873
Ross, Charles Oscar 1889
Shull, Benjamin C. 1886
Smith, Nathan and Emily 1872
Smith, W. D. L. F. 1864
Spires, Lloyd 1890
Warner, Calvin M. 1864
Warner, William 1866
Waterman, C. F. 1899

Curry County

Crook, Edwin 1879
Jensen, Orlinnie 1902
Kreutzer, J. J. 1902
McKenzie, Robert 1874
Moore, Thomas Franklin 1900
Solomon, Sara Culver 1896
Walker, James Gibson and Alpharetta (Zahniser) 1882

Deschutes County

Douglas County

Applegate, Charles 1865
Applegate, Jesse 1857
Arrington, James M. and Kitty Ann C. 1851
Bacon, Henry Nieman and Virginia S. W. 1890
Baimbridge, Thomas 1872
Beckley, Henry 1859
Blakely, Samuel P. 1852
Boone, Synthia Ann and Paris 1849
Brown, Henry G. 1856
Butler, Rufus 1850
Churchhill, Alva and Bernetta 1854
Clayton, Jesse C. 1848
Cowan, Robert 1848
Davlin, James 1867
Doerner, Adam 1889
Dyer, Moses T. 1852
Fate, David 1858
Fortin, Sr., Ferdinand 1869
Gazley, James E. 1851
Gurney, Robert M. and Elizabeth 1853
Hayhurst, William 1857
Henderer, Charles G. and Emeline Meador 1859
Jones, Abraham 1852
Jones, Henry 1852
Jones, John 1858
LaBrie, Ferdinand 1866
LaRaut, Sr., Narcisse 1878
Long, John 1850
Martindale, Alston 1853
Maupin, Martha A. 1868
McCulloch, William T. 1852
McGee, W. D. 1864

McLaughlin, Joseph and Martha	1859
Michaels, Lawrence	1898
Morell, Milan and Mary E. Melvin	1881
Nichols, Israel Boyd	1852
Phipps, Robert Matlock	1851
Putnam, Joseph	1853
Raymond, Ephraim	1883
Rice, Harrison	1856
Sawyers, Andrew	1850
Sheffield, James F.	1858
Singleton, William and Thomas Singleton	1854
Smith, Charles W.	1851
Stephens, Ebenezer	1852
Thomas, Richard	1863
Walker, Alpheus	1874
Walker, Charles F.	1884
Weatherly, Hiram	1882
Weaver, Adam	1873
Weaver, Hans	1867
Wells, Asaph	1852
Wilson, W. H. and Hannah Dickinson	1849

Gilliam County

Bartlemay, William	1901
Dyer, James W.	1893
Froman, Ralph	1884
Hardie, Dave	1883
Little, Charles L.	1882
Madden, John	1882
McKinney, James Madison and Polly Elmira	1881
Mobley, Thomas "Tip"	1872
Nelson, James H. and Elizina E.	1886
Parman, Giles G.	1884
Philippi, Albert	1886
Quinn, Charles J.	1883
Robinson, Robert George	1880
Shannon, Francis Marion	1884
Smith, Frank Eugene	1891
Stinchfield, Edmund A.	1890
Summers, Mary E.	1883
Weatherford, Francis M.	1887
Weimar, John	1886

Grant County

Amacher, Fred, and Ernest F. Ricco, Sr.	1897
Belshaw, Charles	1864
Blackwell, Clement Cood and Jane	1876
Capon, John Urban	1897
Deardorff, Flem and Sara Manwaring	1869
Ingle, William B. "Billy" and Julia	1869
Keerins, David	1890
Keerins, Joseph Henry Grattan and Della Mae	1895
Keerins, Matthew	1895
Keerins, Owen	1886
Kuhl, Peter and Julia	1872
McGirr, Frank and Henrietta	1880
Oliver, Joseph C. and Lizzie	1880
Shaw, Daniel Wesley and Martha Jane	1876
Stone, Wells Wilcott and Eva Livonia	1882
Trowbridge, Bradford Cornelius	1862
Vaughan, Jack	1904

Harney County

Cecil, William Carrol and Logan	1871
Howard, Thomas	1883
Williams, Hyrum "Hyram"	1895

Promotional brochure issued by Gilliam County Opportunity Assn., 1910. Cultural Images collection

Hood River County

Babson, Sydney and Rea	1908
Dethman, Christian	1887
Jackson, Capt. Francis Marion	1871
Kollas, Philip	1894
Lage, Hans	1876
Wells, Jerome	1901

Jackson County

Beeson, John	1853
Birdseye, David Nelson and Clarissa	1852
Brown, Henry R.	1854
Buckley, James David	1854
Carver, Ebenezer W.	1868
Chavner, Thomas	1856
Dean, Nathaniel C.	1851
Dosier, Andrew and Livonia	1876
Dunn, Patrick	1852
Elmore, C. H.	1903
Fitzgerald, Nathaniel D.	1882
Hanley, Michael	1857
Kubli, Kaspar	1857
McKay, John W.	1875
Massal, Sr., William	1880
Myer, W. C.	1870
Nealon, Stephen M.	1883
Offenbacher, Fred and Minnie	1898
Parsons, Reginald H. and Maude	1908
Payne, Champion T.	1869
Peninger, John and Mary Elizabeth	1853
Ross, Col. John E. and Elizabeth	1853

Jefferson County

Bolter, Edward G.	1879
Read, Lillie	1898

Josephine County

White, Samuel Wilson	1855

Klamath County

Campbell, David	1885
Hill, William F.	1894
Horton, William Harrison	1868
Kilgore, Silas Wright	1876
Loosley, John	1873
Owen, James	1879
Pope, Fred L.	1898
Riggs, Elija	1882
Taylor, Samuel H.	1880

Lake County

Brattain, Thomas Jefferson	1877
Corum, Samuel G.	1881
Harvey, William	1880
Withers, Peter	1871

Lane County

Adkins, Edward S.	1851
Bailey, George	1852
Bangs, Frederick and Daisy	1903
Benninger, William James and Ida Florence	1893
Benson, Sarah S.	1851
Bond, Allen and Rachel	1853
Bond, William and Hetty	1853
Brown, John and Nancy Richardson	1848
Cox, Solomon	1852
Deming, Franklin Fayette	1883
Edwards, Isaac N.	1871
Ellmaker, Enos	1857
Ferguson, John B.	1875

Gray, Frederick L.	1861
Hale, Calvin T.	1853
Hale, Captain	1856
Hawley, Ira and Elvira	1852
Hills, Cornelius J.	1847
Humphrey, George W.	1872
Huston, Henry Clay	1853
Inman, Joel C. and Sophia	1852
Jenkins, Stephen	1852
Jensen, Anders	1905
Johnston, James and Mary	1884
Loehner, George	1872
McCulloch, John and Thomas McCulloch	1853
McDole, James Merritt	1881
McFarland, John Ward	1853
Millican, Robert	1865
Mosby, David	1852
Nighswander, Francis Marion	1864
Pitney, John P. and Elizabeth	1855
Porter, John R.	1859
Robinson, L. Richard	1857
Sears, Carrol Jackson	1852
Spores, James Madison	1857
Steinhauer, Herman	1893
Stephens, Sidney S.	1867
Stevens, William	1847
Storment, Alexander Franklin	1868
Thomas, Johnathan and Jeanette	1853
Trunnell, Jesse	1890
Wilkins, Mitchell and Permelia Ann	1847
Woolridge, John	1854
Wright, Fred	1891

Lincoln County

Edwards, Malinda F.	1896
Grant, Benjamin Franklin	1872
Grant, Elijah, II	1898
Wakefield, Louisa	1889

Linn County

Alford, Russell and Martha Jane Rodgers	1851
Barr, Jessie and Anne	1852
Bateman, John	1851
Bellinger, Francis	1850
Bland, Martha and Moses	1859
Bond, Nathan	1850
Brattain, Jonathan H.	1849
Brock, Vineyard C.	1854
Burkhart, Leander C. and Malissa Ann	1847
Carns, William	1852
Chambers, George and Rosetta	1905
Chambers, Matthew C.	1866
Cheadle, Richard	1858
Cochran, William	1848
Cogswell, John	1871
Coon, Washington L.	1850
Cox, Lewis	1848
Crabtree, John J.	1847
Crooks, Samuel T.	1877
Cummings, Martin	1887
Curtis, Palmer	1892
Davidson, Henry	1852
Davidson, Thurston	1875
Davidson, William M.	1874
Evans, Edward	1852
Farwell, Richard and Esther	1852
Fitzwater, James B.	1865
Foster, Robert	1853
Freeland, Edward A.	1871

Promotional brochure issued by Klamath County Chamber of Commerce, 1928.
Cultural Images collection

Freitag, Charles and Matilda	1896
Froman, Isaac R. and Eliza Jane	1852
Gilkey, Allen	1881
Grimes, Beal R.	1866
Groshong, Mary A.	1904
Hamilton, Joseph and Caroline	1848
Hamlin, Willard F.	1891
Hardman, Samuel and Mary	1850
Harrison, Jarvis	1852
Hawley, Ira	1856
Hayworth, John B.	1875
Henness, Thomas J.	1864
Hudel, Jacob Henry	1895
Ingram, William H.	1855
Jackson, Willis Ellis and Mary Rich	1853
Jenks, James Benton	1866
Jones, Samuel T.	1853
Kelly, J. J.	1854
Kennell, C. R.	1890
Ketchum, Walter M. and Laura	1851
Kirk, Henry H.	1860
Kizer, Horton and Mary	1898
Knighten, Commodore P. and Rosanna	1853
Lane, Horace and Margaret	1853
Leever, C. T.	1854
Lines, John and Martha M.	1864
Loat, Edward	1858
Looney, Anthony S.	1865
McFarland, Rueben A.	1852
Meeker, John and Lydia	1848
Miller, Christian	1851
Montgomery, William G. and Mary L.	1855
Morgan, Miller and Elizabeth	1850
Munkers, Preston	1846
Newton, Samuel C.	1862
Ohling, Paul	1871
Overton, George D.	1860
Parrish, Gamaliel	1847
Payne, Martin	1852
Peery, James H. and Charlotte	1870
Penland, Henry	1858
Powell, Joseph Ambrose	1863
Pugh, F. A.	1861
Radir, Adam and Margaret	1875
Reiley, John K.	1852
Rice, James Norval	1853
Richardson, Charles W.	1874
Robnett, William	1848
Rodgers, Milton and Elizabeth	1851
Rose, Andrew Jackson	1865
Russell, Newton and Susan L.	1852
Schick, John	1886
Settle, John	1847
Shedd, Capt. Frank	1865
Shelton, Haman	1847
Sherer, Sarah	1852
Slate, John T. and Frances	1843
Smith, Edward and Angeline	1905
Smith, James A.	1878
Smith, Robert L.	1890
Smith, Thomas Fleming	1875
Sprenger, Nicholas B.	1852
Swank, Phillip	1857
Tandy, Edwin Napper	1871
Tindall, Charles and Ruth Marion	1953
Vance, William L.	1868
Wilkinson, James and Sarah	1875
Wilson, Lewis and Emma	1885

Malheur County

Adams, Isaac Hugh	1881
Duncan, George W. and Susan D.	1880
Jensen, Andrew	1894
Molthan, Summers and Mary Jane	1897
Scott, William J.	1878

Marion County

Anderson, James Mechlin	1847
Bashaw, Joseph	1846
Bauman, Elizabeth	1895
Benson, Charles	1848
Bochsler, Joseph	1890
Brandt Jr., Helmuth Alfred and Meda Hobart	1902
Brotl, Jacob and Virginia	1850
Brown, Samuel and Elizabeth	1850
Brumbaugh, Andrew	1865
Buhr, John and Jacob	1897
Caplinger, Jacob	1845
Claggett, Charles	1852
Cook, John J.	1856
Coolidge, Ai	1856
Coyle, Michael	1855
Davenport, Dr. Benjamin and Sarah	1851
Davidson, James Frederick and Mary Anna	1901
Dickens, Reuben and Nancy	1858
Dimmick, Augustine Right and Laura Ann	1847
Doerfler, Martin	1877
Doty, Nelson R.	1853
Eder, Andress	1876
Edmunson, Rufus C.	1863
Egan, William H.	1875
Eoff, John Leonard	1848
Esson, Alexander and Christina Stevens	1861
Etzel, Joseph and Katerina	1896
Ferschweiler, Peter J. and Elizabeth	1873
Fisher, Joseph	1879
Geelan, Patrick	1864
Geer, R. C. and Mary C.	1848
Gerig, Peter	1892
Gooding, Nicholas	1894
Goodknecht, Peter	1881
Hadley, Jesse Hershel	1871
Hafner, John	1907
Hassler, Joseph	1892
Heater, Lorenzo Dow	1852
Hibbard, K. L.	1878
Hovenden, Amos	1874
Hunsaker, Thomas H.	1858
Hunt Sr., Thomas J.	1847
Hunt, George Washington	1850
Johns, John A. and Julia A.	1852
Jones, Fielding and Martha	1847
Jones, S. W. R.	1854
Jones, Silas and Sally	1849
Keil, Fredrick	1856
King, Jane	1860
King, John	1849
King, Thomas and Harriette	1849
Kinyon, J. R. and L. A.	1887
Kirk, John, and Thomas Kirk	1878
Kulzer, Joseph	1895
Lichty, Nicholas	1878
Lieber, John	1857
Loe, Ole and Ragnild	1902
Looney, Jessie and Reuby	1850
Manning, Francis	1857
McCormick, Matthew	1869
McKay, James	1856
McKay, James and Cecilia	1848

Cover of promotional pamphlet, issued by Sheridan Commercial Club and Southern Pacific Co., 1909. Cultural Images collection

Miller Sr., Henry and Celine Eckerlin	1888
Miller, George B.	1855
Miller, Isaac	1848
Minto, John and Martha Ann	1846
Moisan, Thomas and Harriet	1842
Morris, William and Elizabeth	1850
Mulkey, Charles J.	1850
Norton, T. H.	1851
Pendleton, D. J.	1850
Porter, William	1848
Prantl, John and Mary	1874
Ramp, Samuel	1856
Raymond, Augustin (or Remon)	1840
Reeves, Bartley	1854
Riches, George P. S. and Mary J.	1849
Ryan, Joseph J.	1875
Savage, John M. and Jane	1850
Schiedler, Joseph and Kathrina	1875
Schifferer, John Philipp	1893
Schindler, Leonard	1850
Shaw, George W. and Jane	1851
Short, John W.	1858
Simmons, Asa B.	1866
Singer, John	1888
Skaife, John and Mariette	1854
Smith, John F.	1857
Stauffer Sr., John	1872
Stauffer, Jacob and Josephine Gerig	1892
Stevens, Hanson	1852
Stout, Lewis	1852
Tate, William H.	1878
Thompson, Alexander	1868
West, Ashby	1876
White, Thomas J.	1866
White, Virginia (Brotyl)	1852
Williamson, Nelson P.	1884
Yergen, August	1855

Morrow County

Bartholomew, Harry, and Charles Bartholomew	1898
Becket, J. W.	1886
Bergstrom, Erick	1900
Bergstrom, Olof	1887
Brosnan, Jeremiah	1875
Brundage, Walter S., and Albert W. Osmin	1888
Carlson, Andrew S. and Sophia	1883
Devin, Mifflin Jay and Sara Elizabeth Devin	1884
Doherty, James G.	1891
Hamer, Jesse	1873
Huston, Luther	1885
Kenny, Michael and Mary	1883
Lindsay, John and Catherine Anne Kincaid	1884
McMillan, E. D.	1892
Mullally, John and Catherine	1889
Olden, Menzo Alfred	1884
Palmer, Lawrence A.	1900
Peck, Clinton North	1888
Peterson, John E.	1891
Reitmann, Paul	1883
Stevens, Robert	1904
Thomson, Henry Clay	1871
Wright, Albert	1873
Wright, Anson E.	1881
Wright, Anson Evan	1889

Multnomah County

Bell, Ulysses Grant and Etta Bates	1889
Benfield, Frederick and Charlotte	1877

Brooks, David	1876
Butler, Euphemia	1878
Carlson, Gust and Mathilda	1905
Charlton, Joseph and Margaret C.	1848
Graf, Andreas	1881
Jenne, Lemuel and Susan	1858
Kerslake, Allen	1904
Kerslake, Robert	1893
Kruger, Louisa	1883
McIntire, Horace and Narcissa	1851
Morgan, Edward	1849
Moulton, George Frederick	1875
Powell, Dr. and Mrs. John Parker	1853
Powell, Jackson	1855
Reeder, Simon M.	1853
Stanley, Jeremiah	1853
Williams, T. K.	1853

Polk County

Allen, John Ceton and Nancy Catherine McNary	1851
Ball, Isaac and Abigail	1850
Baskett, George	1857
Bell, George Cyrus and Mary Ann DeLong	1852
Billings, George and Emma	1858
Blair, Thomas R. and Emmaline Buell	1848
Brunk, Harrison	1858
Buhler, Jacob B.	1893
Domes, Albert	1892
Fawk, John	1868
Fishback, John L.	1890
Flickinger, Henry	1856
Ford, Nathaniel and Lucinda D.	1858
Frizzell, G. L. and Alice A.	1890
Frizzell, Lillian	1853
Gardner, Samuel J.	1844
Gilliam, Andrew Jackson	1847
Gregg, Noah F.	1884
Griffith, B. L.	1867
Guy, Mahlon	1875
Hill, Henry Washington and Martha Ann	1847
Mulkey, James Huston	1883
Peters, David	1903
Phillips, John and Elizabeth	1847
Porterfield, Amax	1853
Powell, Franklin S.	1874
Read, Hankerson and Jane Read	1853
Riddell, William, and David Rae	1875
Ridgeway, John	1846
Riggs, James B.	1845
Ritner, Sebastian R. and Sarah	1844
Savage, William	1845
Savage, William and Mary Christina	1853
Simon, W. F. Talbernina	1902
Smith, Absalom and Hylah	1848
Stump, David	1860
Tharp, Abraham and Margaret	1866
Vandevort, William	1859
Walker, Claybourne C. and Louisa	1845
Walker, Harvey and Hannah J.	1889
Windsor, Benjamin F.	1868

Sherman County

Andrews, Charles M.	1892
Fridley, George Calvin	1888
Hilderbrand, George W.	1894
Kaseberg, John C.	1882
King, Presley	1886
Martin, Leroy H. and Amanda	1886
McDermid, John D.	1890
Medler, Bruno F.	1901

ROSTER OF OREGON CENTURY FARMS & RANCHES SINCE 1958

Medler, Henry	1889
Moore, Helen and John A.	1881
Pinkerton, Robert W.	1893
Powell, William	1895
Richelderfer, Henry	1888
Sayrs, Frank Alroy	1883
Starns, Robert Middleton	1889
Strong, Horace	1896
Thompson, Charles W.	1890
Van Gilder, Milon	1898
Van Patten, Francies	1885
von Borstel, Carsten	1886

Tillamook County

Alley, John Marshall	1882
Bailey, David A.	1895
Craven, John K.	1886
Donaldson, Joseph G	1864
Elliott, Margaret F.	1882
Rock, Samuel Hardy	1876
Vaughn, Warren	1852
Weber, John	1898
Wyss, Gottlieb and Susann	1898

Umatilla County

Adams, John Franklin	1865
Beauchamp, Isadore	1879
Brown, William, Jr.	1886
Coppock, Robert	1878
Davis, John A.	1880
Demaris, Enoch	1884
Denninge, Mathias	1883
Doherty, Pat	1906
Dougherty, Robert W. and Elizabeth	1903
Duff, David	1889
Eggers, Henry G. F.	1891
Elam, Andrew Martin	1880
Enbysk, Peter Christian	1877
Estoup, Michael	1876
Gilliland, Thomas Pence	1904
Hales, Hugh Byron Americus	1877
Heidenrich, Lawrence	1898
Hellberg, Christian and Wilhelmina	1908
Hemphill, James Monroe	1865
Holdman Brothers: Oro, Frank, Wade, William	1882
Hudemann, Julius	1889
Jack, Marion	1889
Johnson, Alick	1898
Kern, C.A.	1893
Key, Joe and Ruth	1891
Kopp, John, and Franz Kopp	1898
Kramer, Jacob	1891
Lee, Hiram Benoni	1873
Lieuallen, Josiah	1864
Lieuallen, William	1864
Lorenzen, John Henry	1894
Lynch, John	1876
McAlavy, Charles	1898
McCarty, David and Elizabeth	1878
Miller, Gottlieb	1893
Muller, Louis	1892
Mumm, Jurgen	1879
Nelson, D. H. and Maria Molstrom	1904
Newtson, Newt	1887
O'Hara, Daniel	1862
Olsen, Salve	1888
Pambrum, Andrew Dominique	1879
Peters, John H.	1902
Rencken, Gevert	1903
Rosenberg, Claus H.	1882
Roumagoux, Francis F.	1885

Sams, Peter	1877
Schrimpf, William	1887
Schubert, Jacob	1901
Scott, William H. H.	1872
Shafer, James Wesley	1882
Shaw, Daniel	1890
Shumway, James S.	1870
Swaggart, A. Lincoln and Mary Van Cleave	1889
Teel, John and Elvira	1893
Temple, William R.	1884
Vey, Antone and Mary	1861
Whittaker, Henry	1879
Winn, Ambrose	1898
Winn, Jesse Z.	1875

Union County

Anson, William, George and Joseph	1862
Case, William Jasper	1901
Conley, A. B.	1891
Counsell, Frank	1905
Courtney, Thomas Benton	1868
Davis, John S.	1872
Follett, Warren K.	1905
Gekeler, George O.	1862
Glenn, Tobert T.	1868
Good, John Porter	1890
Gray, George Grant	1872
Halley, Benjamin	1864
Hindman, W. B.	1872
Hutchinson, James	1865
Jasper, Merrel C.	1868
Kelsey, Lorenzo S.	1888
McDonald, Hiram	1873
McKinnis, John L.	1871
Miller, Herman and Flores	1903
Miller, Simon	1863

Morris, Rascellas	1896
Moss, James and Martha Jane Wallsinger	1885
Riggs, James and Maria	1896
Rynearson, William, and John Rynearson	1864
Sanderson, Mathew and Euphemia	1900
Smock, William Lovejoy	1906
Speckhart, John	1904
Standley, James Henry	1870
Van Blokland, John	1890
Wade, Pharris	1883
Wilson, James B.	1889
Woodell, James Lorenzo and Isabel Murchison	1868
Zurbrick, Franklin	1900

Wallowa County

Applegate, Albert	1883
Bacon, Lorenzo	1884
Beach, William Joseph	1890
Chenoweth, James Wesley	1893
Coon, Alice Heller Cannon	1884
Courtney, Alphon and Lucy	1897
Davis, James Francis	1897
Hayes, John W.	1880
Huffman, John W.	1888
Kooch, David	1877
Lathrop, Thomas Madden	1889
McAlister, James W.	1884
Moore, William A.	1897
Nobles, James B.	1888
Pratt, Ira C.	1896
Wade, Samuel	1874
Wolfe, Capt. Gideon	1897
Wood, George D.	1884

ROSTER OF OREGON CENTURY FARMS & RANCHES SINCE 1958

Promotional brochure issued by Oregon Railway & Navigation Co. and Sunset Magazine Homeseekers' Bureau, 1909. Cultural Images collection

Wasco County

Bolton, Absolum	1858
Cooper, Robert	1869
Creighton, David C.	1862
Dickson, Enoch C.	1894
Fargher, Horatio A.	1876
Gray, Yancey	1876
Harvey, Elsie J. and Davis A.	1880
Ingels, Patrick C.	1879
Johnson, Joel C.	1888
Kelly, Hampton	1879
Magill, John B.	1874
Marsh, Josiah	1854
McClure, Thomas J.	1866
McGreer, Thomas Henry	1886
Mesplie, Theodore	1851
Root, Amos	1878
Slusher, Thomas W. Scott and Arabelle Dufur	1861

Washington County

Alexander, George	1871
Bailey, John R.	1891
Bateman, Charles	1884
Bateman, Swanton S.	1885
Beringer, William R.	1893
Bischof, Joseph	1872
Bishop, Henry	1872
Bowlby, Dr. Wilson	1853
Brown, Alvin C.	1850
Cawrse, Joseph	1875
Connell, Joseph, II and Mildred Wood	1886
Connell, Joseph	1874
Cummins, Erwin	1861
Davis, Eli	1847
Demmin, Hulder J.	1884
Denney, Thomas H.	1848
Doris, Eli and Mary Ann	1846
Duyck, Henry and Helen	1907
Eischen, Mathias	1887
Evans, Peter	1880
Fanno, August J.	1847
Flint, B. T.	1865
Gates, John Wesley and Minnie M.	1897
Gembella, August	1895
Haase, Henry	1897
Hahn, Marshall Washington	1875
Harris, George	1874
Hayward, James	1853
Ireland, Robert	1852
Jackson, Ulyses	1878
Johnson, John W.	1879
Jurgens, William	1869
Koehnke, John	1898
Krahmer, Sr., Edward	1877
Langer, Ferdinand	1879
Lee, James A.	1861
Lewis, Franklin James	1905
Lilly, James Pisarius	1884
Marsh, John	1852
Meek, Stephen A. D., and Joseph Lane Meek	1890
Meyer, George M. C.	1883
Mulloy, Alfred D.	1872
Nyberg, John	1895
Papenberg, George	1866
Pearson, Henry Caswell	1892
Pieren, John and Elizabeth	1890
Porter, John	1857
Raffety, Samuel B.	1850
Rieben, Christian	1889
Roberts, Henry Clay	1853

Robinson, William J.	1852
Rowell, Ziba M.	1853
Schlegal, John, and John Schlegal, Jr.	1890
Schlichting, John (Johann)	1878
Schmeltzer, Conrad K.	1878
Schmidt, Fred	1902
Schulmerich, Conrad	1875
Seth, Thomas	1857
Sewell, Henry	1852
Shearer, James N.	1883
Siegenthaler, Samuel	1876
Simpson, John Marshall	1878
Sorenson, Johann and Maren	1881
Unger, Frank	1906
Vanderzanden, John	1881
Walter, Julius and Caroline	1890
Wilcox, Sanford Elias	1849
Williams, Richard	1855
Withycombe, James	1871
Wren, Michael	1846
Wunderlich, Carl and Elizabeth	1896
Yungen, Abraham	1890
Zimmerman, George B.	1883

Wheeler County

Jackson, Martin Joseph	1892
Mulvahill, Abby	1897

Yamhill County

Alderman, Albert L.	1846
Allan, Solomon	1847
Barrett, John	1894
Belt, George C.	1890
Blair, William	1866
Brutscher, Mary Everest and Sebastian	1850
Carl, Wilson	1862
Cary, J. J.	1875
Chapman, William	1852
Christensen, Jeppe	1902
Conner, Nathan and Elizabeth Buell	1848
Cooper, Thomas	1873
Coovert, Abram and Martha	1852
Crimmins, John	1866
Davis, Thomas Crawford	1849
Dundas, James, Jr.	1879
Edwards, Edmond and Christena	1904
Everest, Richard and Jane	1852
Fendall, Charles E. and Amanda	1850
Fletcher, Francis	1858
Flint, Nelson	1888
Freeman, Fred and Margaret	1906
Fryer, Alexander	1863
Goodrich, William	1848
Grahm, William	1849
Grauer, Jacob and Rose	1899
Gubser, Daniel	1891
Gutbrod, George	1894
Gutbrod, George, and Jacob Grauer	1893
Hagey, Levi	1847
Harrison, Thaddus R. and Marie A	1850
Heater, Benjamin and Mary Jane	1850
Hewitt, Henry and Elizabeth Matheny	1843
Hutt, Thomas B.	1848
Jernstedt, Frank Theodore	1885
Keaton, Robert	1856
Kinney, Samuel	1849
Kirkwood, Fred	1899
Lamson, Jeramiah	1847
Laughlin, William and Phoebe	1858
Martin, Nehemiah and Eliza Lois	1850

ROSTER OF OREGON CENTURY FARMS & RANCHES SINCE 1958

Matheny, Daniel	1843	
McKee, John W.	1889	
Morris, Eliam	1852	
Murray, Charles	1852	
Owens, Thomas	1849	
Parrett, Samuel and Maria Everest	1853	
Parrish, Jesse	1853	
Payne, Joshua	1847	
Perkins, Eli and Sally Hull	1844	
Phillips, Richard W.	1861	
Robinson, Benjamin M. and Elizabeth J. Chrisman	1845	
Rowland, Jeremiah	1844	
Russell, William S.	1899	
Sawyer, Mark and Susan James	1847	
Scott, John C. and Sally Harper	1874	
Sitton, N. K.	1845	
Smith, Darling	1859	
Smith, Ella Parrett	1903	
Stout, Jonathan	1864	
Tharp, Abraham	1857	
Wenger, Rudolph	1889	
Winters, Phillip and Polly	1852	
Yocom, Jesse	1847	
Youngberg, Nels B. and Hannah	1889	
Zimmerman, Christian and Cecilia	1883	

Farmer's shipping tag, about 1930. Author's collection

SESQUICENTENNIAL FARMS & RANCHES

CLACKAMAS COUNTY
Hattan, Mark A.	1847
Trullinger, Gabriel and Sarah	1852
Vaughan, William Hatchette	1844

JACKSON COUNTY
Birdseye, David N. and Clarissa	1852

LANE COUNTY
Brown, John and Nancy	1848
Hawley, Ira and Elvira	1852
Jenkins, Stephen	1852

LINN COUNTY
Brock, Vineyard C.	1854
Coon, Washington L.	1850
Jackson, Willis E. and Mary Rich	1853
Montgomery, William G. and Mary L.	1855
Rice, James Norval	1853
Sprenger, Nicholas B.	1852

MARION COUNTY
Davenport, Dr. Benjamin and Sarah	1851
Heater, Lorenzo Dow	1852
King, John	1849
McKay, James	1856

YAMHILL COUNTY
Goodrich, William	1848
Rowland, Jeremiah	1844

Index to recipes
Recipes are indexed by title, by main ingredient, and by type of dish

All-purpose spray cleaner, 96
Amanda's navy bean chowder, 18

Apples
Caramel nut apple pie, 61
English boiled pudding, 70
Favorite applesauce cake, 74
Fresh apple cake, 79
German apple cobbler, 62
Grandma Carrie Hobart's apple fritters, 50

Aunt Gretchen's chewie dewies, 80
Aunt Helen's fruit pudding, 64

Bananas
Fluffy banana cake, 72
Zetta's banana bread, 48

Bangs family breakfast sausage, 30

Beans
Amanda's navy bean chowder, 18
3-bean chili in crock pot, 24

Beef
Beef Stroganoff, 26
Come and get it, 25
Fantastic five-hour stew, 31
Hay season round steak, 27
Italian sausage, 36
Italian stuffed cabbage, 38
Meat loaf, 31
Paula's stir-fry peppers, beef and cabbage, 32
Russian cabbage rolls, 40
Seared sirloin strips with dried tomatoes and mushrooms, 34
Sue's Mexican lasagna, 28
Swiss steak, 35

Tamale pie, 33
3-bean chili in crock pot, 24

Beets
Velma Hiatt Laughlin's pickled beets, 11

Blackberries
Crow's nest pudding, 60
Famous Ella Allen raisin pudding, 68
Fresh raspberry cake, 83
Old-time favorite fruit cobbler, 67

Blueberries
Blueberry oatmeal cookies, 90

Boiled fruit cake, 76
Boiled spice cake (Depression cake), 75

Boysenberries
see Blackberries

Bran flax
Charlene's bran flax muffins, 46

Bread pudding (sponsor), 41

Breads
Swedish flat bread (knäckebröd), 47
Zetta's banana bread, 48

Broccoli salad, 22

Cabbage
Cabbage-shrimp salad, 14
Italian stuffed cabbage, 38
Paula's stir-fry peppers, beef and cabbage, 32
Russian cabbage rolls, 40
Sauerkraut salad, 20

Cakes
Aunt Gretchen's chewie dewies, 80
Boiled fruit cake, 76
Boiled spice cake (Depression cake), 75
Favorite applesauce cake, 74
Fluffy banana cake, 72
Fresh apple cake, 79
Fresh raspberry cake, 83
Lois Hiatt Parrish's prune cake, 81
Love cake, 5
Maple bars, 82
Old Jacksonville white cake, 77
Welsh tea cakes, 51
Whipped cream cake, 73

Caramel nut apple pie, 61

Casseroles
Come and get it, 25
Gourmet scalloped potatoes, 34 (sponsor)
Hay season round steak, 26
Mom's mac'n'cheese for a crowd, 29
Sue's Mexican lasagna, 28
Tamale pie, 33

Charlene's bran flax muffins, 46

Cheese
Impossible quiche, 30
Mom's mac'n'cheese for a crowd, 29

Cherries
Hood River brandied cherries, 86
Ways to use cherries, 86

121

Index to recipes

Chili
  3-bean chili in crock pot, 24
Cleaner
  All-purpose spray cleaner, 96
Cobblers
  German apple cobbler, 62
  Marionberry cobbler, 69
  Old-time favorite fruit cobbler, 67
Come and get it, 25
Cookies
  Aunt Gretchen's chewie dewies, 80
  Blueberry oatmeal cookies, 90
  Dream puffs, 91
  Ginger snaps, 88
  Grandma's oatmeal cookies, 89
  Great Grandma Smith's sugar cookies, 84
  Lemon bars, 87
  Nut wafer cookies, 92
  Oatmeal chip cookies, 78
Cream pie
  Old timers cream pie, 56
Creamed peas and potatoes, 42
Crow's nest pudding, 60
Curried fruit, 58

Depression cake
  Boiled spice cake (Depression cake), 75
Dill dip, 10
Dips
  Oyster dip, 12

Dill dip, 10
Dream puffs, 91
Dressings, salad see Salad dressings
Dry roasted hazelnuts, 97
Ducks
  To catch wild ducks, 98

Elderberry soup, 15
English boiled pudding, 75

Famous Ella Allen raisin pudding, 68
Fantastic five-hour stew, 31
Favorite applesauce cake, 74
Filberts see Hazelnuts
Fluffy banana cake, 72
French toast
  Holiday French toast, 52
Fresh apple cake, 79
Fresh raspberry cake, 83
Fritters
  Grandma Carrie Hobart's apple fritters, 50

Frostings see Icings
Fruit salads see Salads

German apple cobbler, 62
Ginger snaps, 88
Gooseberries
  Aunt Helen's fruit pudding, 64
Gourmet scalloped potatoes, 29 (sponsor)
Grammy Jane's buttermilk salad, 17

Grandma Carrie Hobart's apple fritters, 50
Grandma Christine's creamed peas and new potatoes, 43
Grandma Marie's lefse, 49
Grandma's oatmeal cookies, 89
Gravy
  Perfect gravy every time, 20
Great Grandma Smith's sugar cookies, 84

Ham
  Marie Schubert's ham loaf, 27
Hay season round steak, 27
Hazelnuts
  Caramel nut apple pie, 61
  Dry roasted hazelnuts, 97
  Vernon's favorite glazed hazelnuts, 84
Holiday French toast, 52
Homemade lye soap, 99
Hood River brandied cherries, 86

Icings
  Irene's angel food cake icing, 93
  Maple icing, 82
  Pink raspberry frosting, 83
Impossible quiche, 30
Irene's angel food cake icing, 93
Italian sausage, 36
Italian stuffed cabbage, 38

Judy's rosa marina fruit salad, 16

Knäckebröd
Swedish flat bread (knäckebröd), 47

Lasagna
Sue's Mexican lasagna, 28

Lefse
Grandma Marie's lefse, 49

Lemon bars, 87

Lois Hiatt Parrish's prune cake, 81

Lola Offenbacher's dill pickles, 9

Love cake, 5

Macaroni
Mom's mac'n'cheese for a crowd, 29

Maple bars, 82

Maple icing, 82

Marie Schubert's ham loaf, 27

Marionberry cobbler, 69

Marionberries see also Blackberries

Mary Jane's strawberry preserves, 55

Meat loaf, 31

Mom's mac'n'cheese for a crowd, 29

Mom's rhubarb cream pie, 54

Muffins
Charlene's bran flax muffins, 46

Nano's mustard sauce, 14

Nut wafer cookies, 92

Oatmeal chip cookies, 78

Old German style pickles, 9

Old Jacksonville white cake, 77

Old-time favorite fruit cobbler, 67

Old timers cream pie, 56

Oyster dip, 12

Paula's butternut squash soup, 19

Paula's stir-fry peppers, beef and cabbage, 32

Peaches
Old-time favorite fruit cobbler, 67

Peanut butter playdough, 96

Pearfection, 65

Pears
Pearfection, 65

Rustic pear tart (sponsor), 59

Peas
Creamed peas and potatoes, 42

Grandma Christine's creamed peas and new potatoes, 43

To shell large batch of fresh peas, 98

Perfect gravy every time, 20

Pickles
Green tomato relish, 8

Lola Offenbacher's dill pickles, 9

Old German style pickes, 9

Velma Hiatt Laughlin's pickled beets, 11

Pies
Caramel nut apple pie, 61

Impossible quiche, 30

Mom's rhubarb cream pie, 54

Old timers cream pie, 56

Strawberry pie, 63

Tamale pie, 33

Pink raspberry frosting, 83

Playdough
Peanut butter playdough, 96

Plums (Fresh Prunes)
Prune conserve, 57

Pork
Bangs family breakfast sausage, 30

Italian sausage, 36

Marie Schubert's ham loaf, 27

Russian cabbage rolls, 40

Verboort sausage, 35

Potato dumplings, 39

Potatoes
Creamed peas and potatoes, 42

Gourmet scalloped potatoes, 34 (sponsor)

Grandma Christine's creamed peas and new potatoes, 43

Grandma Marie's lefse, 49

Potato dumplings, 39

Preserves
Hood River brandied cherries, 86

Mary Jane's strawberry preserves, 55

Prune conserve, 57

Strawberry sun jam, 66

Prune conserve, 57

Prunes
Lois Hiatt Parrish's prune cake, 81

Prune conserve, 57

Puddings
Aunt Helen's fruit pudding, 64

Crow's nest pudding, 60

Index to recipes

Curried fruit, 58
English boiled pudding, 70
Famous Ella Allen raisin pudding, 68
Rhubarb pudding, 57

Raisins
Boiled fruit cake, 76
Boiled spice cake (Depression cake), 75
Famous Ella Allen raisin pudding, 68

Raspberries
Fresh raspberry cake, 83
Pink raspberry frosting, 83

Relishes
Green tomato relish, 8

Rhubarb
Aunt Helen's fruit pudding, 64
Mom's rhubarb cream pie, 54
Rhubarb pudding, 57
Rhubarb pudding, 57
Russian cabbage rolls, 40
Rustic pear tart (sponsor), 59

Salad dressings
Broccoli salad, 22
Nano's mustard sauce, 14
Sauerkraut salad, 20

Salads
Broccoli salad, 22
Cabbage-shrimp salad, 14
Grammy Jane's buttermilk salad, 17
Judy's rosa marina fruit salad, 16
Sauerkraut salad, 20

Sauces
Nano's mustard sauce, 14

Sauerkraut
Sauerkraut, 39
Sauerkraut salad, 20

Sausage
Bangs family breakfast sausage, 30
Italian sausage, 36
Italian stuffed cabbage, 38
Verboort sausage, 35
Seared sirloin strips with dried tomatoes and mushrooms, 34

Shrimp
Cabbage-shrimp salad, 14

Soap
Homemade lye soap, 99

Soups
Amanda's navy bean chowder, 18
Elderberry soup, 15
Paula's butternut squash soup, 19
Summer garden soup, 21

Squash
Paula's butternut squash soup, 19

Stews
Fantastic five-hour stew, 31

Strawberries
Mary Jane's strawberry preserves, 55
Strawberry pie, 63
Strawberry sun jam, 66
Sue's Mexican lasagna, 28
Summer garden soup, 21
Swedish flat bread (knäckebröd), 47

Sweets
Aunt Gretchen's chewie dewies, 80
Curried fruit, 58
Grandma Carrie Hobart's apple fritters, 50
Grandma Marie's lefse, 49
Holiday French toast, 52
Maple bars, 82
Rhubarb pudding, 57
Welsh tea cakes, 51
Swiss steak, 35

Tamale pie, 33
3-bean chili in crock pot, 24
To catch wild ducks, 98
To shell large batch of fresh peas, 98

Tomatoes
Green tomato relish, 8

Velma Hiatt Laughlin's pickled beets, 11
Verboort sausage, 35
Vernon's favorite g lazed hazelnuts, 84

Walnuts
Boiled fruit cake, 76
Nut wafer cookies, 92
Welsh tea cakes, 51
Whipped cream cake, 73

Zetta's banana bread, 48